In Combat with the Blackhawks

Blessings

from
Those Days of Battle

Sidney A. Hatch, Th. M.

Copyright © 1996
by Josephine A. Hatch

Hatch, Sidney A.
   In combat with the Blackhawks: blessings from those days of
battle / by Sidney A. Hatch.
   p. cm.
   Includes bibliographical references.
   Preassigned LCCN: 96-85661
   ISBN 0-939116-43-X

   1. Hatch, Sidney A. 2.World War, 1939-1945--Personal
narratives, American. 3. United States. Army. Infantry Division,
86th. 4. World War, 1939-1945--Campaigns--Western front. I.
Title.

   D811.H38 1996   940.54'1273

                         QBI96-40212

Published by Frontier Publishing
Portland, OR 97233

For order fulfillment contact your distributors and whole-
salers, or
                    Josephine Hatch
              21800 S.W. Pacific Highway, #41
                 Sherwood, OR 97140-9130

Printed in the United States of America

Foreword

By Dr. John F. Wood
86th Blackhawk Infantry Division

There is a common experience which draws together and holds human beings in an uncommon bond. Enduring and surviving extraordinarily difficult and traumatic events uniquely cements families and friends in peace and in war. Witness the "stick togetherness" of siblings who triumph over difficult childhoods or the popularity of the various Armed Services annually celebrating victory. In contrast note the isolation among Vietnam veterans who endured the double trauma of not enjoying military triumph over the enemy and then returning home in disappointment.

Memories of these bonds, forged in war and branded upon the heart, unexpectedly tugged at me again when I came across a letter to the editor in our metropolitan paper written by a "Rev. Sidney A. Hatch." An immediate phone call re-established a friendship which began nearly a half-century ago in a Louisiana swampland boot camp. Sid Hatch and the soldiers of this book experienced, endured and survived World War II. The seven of our comrades who did not survive the war endure in our memory and the bond remains.

Fifty years have passed and the bond still holds.

Our infantry unit is credited with forty-two days of front line combat in Europe. We defined the front lines as that pencil line scrawled on the battle map before which was no one but the enemy. Not seen on the map are the conditions under which one shares very easily with his buddy to the right his chocolate bar, his buddy on the left his canteen. Here one shares both his fragile dreams and his solid hopes— even his innermost being.

A flood of memories return as I devour these pages. I vividly recall my idol, Captain Hensley. I see Jimmy Curtis. I remember Sid Hatch. This proud reader knows that as you read *In Combat with the Blackhawks, Blessings from Those Days of Battle* you will sense these human bonds. You will be able to understand the character of the author and know why he was the most respected and admired noncommissioned officer that Ol' Easy Company ever had.

John J. Wood, D.O., M.D.

Preface

"In charity to all mankind, bearing no malice or ill-will to any human being."[1]

–John Quincy Adams (July 30, 1838)

This book is about spiritual experiences in combat during World War II. The events related here may not have seemed spiritual when they occurred–very few of them did–but in the years that followed, and in moments of reflection, I realized their impact upon my life.

The term "spiritual" is used here rather broadly. An experience in combat may have affected my relationship to God or it may have influenced my attitude toward other human beings, whether friend or foe.

This is also a book of essays, most of them short and most of them originally written to stand alone. Some of them have appeared in *Brief Bible Studies*, a periodical I have been writing for many years. Two of these experiences have appeared in print elsewhere. They are all included now, with revisions, in this collection.

The events recorded here are not necessarily in chronological order. We were not permitted to keep diaries lest they fall into the hands of the enemy. After fifty years a strict chronology is beyond the memory of this writer. Several of the chapters span the entire period of our time in Germany and Austria, even a little before and after.

I have, however, made some attempt at a chronological presentation. It will take us from the high seas of the North Atlantic to the beautiful hills of the Austrian Tyrol. I close with the story of my return to a village I could not forget.

These experiences are written as I remember them. Nevertheless I am indebted to several individuals who helped jog my memory. They are Dr. John F. Wood, D.O., M.D., of Cornelius, Oregon; Mr. Robert M. Chase of Hampdem, Maine; The Reverend Phil C. McLain of Marietta, Georgia; and Mr. Ira R. Young of White Sulphur Springs, West Virginia. We went through "the valley of the shadow of death" together. Their help came through material they had written, personal correspondence,or private conversation. However, I assume responsibility for the accuracy or inaccuracy of this book's contents.

Richard Kent Matthews, who edited this book, was invaluable to its publication.. I deeply appreciate his very professional help and guidance.

Several publications have proven helpful to me. First, and most important, is a series of articles written by members of our infantry company and compiled in pamphlet form under the title, "You Ain't Seen Nothin' Yet." Included among the writers are Dr. John F. Wood and Mr. Robert M. Chase mentioned above.

"You Ain't Seen Nothin' Yet" was written in the Philippines after the close of hostilities in both Europe and the Pacific. It traces the history of Company "E" of the 342nd Infantry Regiment from its origin at Camp Howze, Texas, in 1942 until its deployment to the Philippines in August of 1945 with the 86th Division. There early in 1946, while memories were fresh and records available, this valuable document was composed.

Other publications which have proven helpful to me are:

86th Blackhawk Infantry Division (Padducah, Ky.: Turner Publishing Company, 1992). 120 pages, with text by Philip A. St. John, Ph.D.

Richard A. Briggs, *Black Hawks Over the Danube, The History of the 86th Infantry Division in World War II* (West point, Ky.: Richard A. Briggs, 1954), 127 pages.

Richard A. Briggs, *The Battle of the Ruhr Pocket, A Combat Narrative* (West Point, Ky.: Richard A. Briggs, 1957), 84 pages.

I must also express appreciation to David C. Cook Publishing Company of Elgin, Illinois (850 N. Grow Ave., 60120). I first told the story of the wounded German soldier who said, *"Du bist wie eine Mutter,"* in my article "The Night I Overcame My enemy," which appeared in *Sunday Digest* for September 5, 1965. It is told here again with their permission.

A few of the photographs in the ETO were obtained from Milo F. Williams of Co. F. We appreciate them, but have not been able to locate him at this time for his permission for their use in this book.

I think it is safe to say that when the average person returns from military service, especially combat, they prefer to concentrate on "forgetting those things which are behind, and reaching forth unto those things which are before."[3] Yet they share a few things with loved ones and friends. This was my experience. Some of the events related here were told at first only to family members. In those years immediately following World War II it seemed that almost everybody was a veteran or had been involved in the war effort in some way. Very few of us felt that our experiences were unique.

After entering the Christian ministry I came to use some of these stories as illustrations. Even then a certain diffidence and restraint was necessary. A congregation can soon tire of the pastor's "war stories."

However, as the years went by and my family grew older, my wife, Jo, and our four children urged me to put some of these stories into writing. I finally succumbed, though willingly, to the pressure.

"It was a valuable experience but I wouldn't want to go through it again." No one uses that cliche more than the veteran; nevertherless it is true. I would add this thought, drawing again upon the words of the apostle Paul: "We know that all things work together for good to them that love God, to them who are the called according to his purpose."[4] A combat experience may not seem conducive to the spiritual life, but God can make the difference.

Finally, though it may seem presumptuous, I want these stories to contribute to binding up the wounds of the past. I feel no malice toward any human being, friend or apparent foe, and I have learned the intrinsic value in the words of Jesus of Nazareth, "Love ye your enemies, and do good ... and ye shall be the children of the Highest."[5]

Unless otherwise indicated, Scripture quotations are from the King James Version of the Bible.

From left: Dr. John F. Wood, Sidney Hatch, Robert M. Chase

Dedication

To my beloved wife
Josephine Bertheau Hatch
who waited patiently and prayerfully at home

and

To my comrades in combat in World War II
Members of Company "E," 342nd Infantry Regiment
86th "Blackhawk" Division

Table of Contents

Part Two: *In the Ruhr*

Part Three: *Across Bavaria with General Patton*

About the Author

Sidney A. ("Sid") Hatch was born in Arizona and grew up in Southern California. He lived in Sherwood, Oregon, until his death October 1, 1995.

He was a graduate of UCLA, the California Baptist Theological Seminary (American Baptist Seminary of the West), and the Dallas Theological Seminary, later earning a General Secondary Credential at the University of Southern California, and a Certificate in Article Writing from Writer's Digest Schools in Cincinnati, Ohio.

Sidney A. Hatch

During World War II Sid served as a sergeant in the 86th Infantry Division (the "Blackhawks") which saw action in Europe and the Philippines. For this service he earned the Combat Infantryman Badge and the Bronze Star Medal.

Except for brief stints at school teaching, Sid spent most of his adult life in the Christian ministry. He pastored churches in California, Texas, Oregon, and Connecticut. He and his wife Josephine ("Jo"), also a graduate of UCLA and a successful school teacher, have four grown children, David, Margaret, Thomas, and Phyllis.

Part I

"In the Beginning"

Introduction

A Spiritual Crisis

"Being confident of this very thing, that he which hath begun a good work in you will perform it until the day of Jesus Christ."

—Philippians 1:6

A lone figure walked hurriedly in our direction. He kept shouting something I couldn't understand.

As the figure drew closer, I recognized him as the student who roomed across the hall from me in the men's dormitory. His message slowly became clearer, something about "Japan ... bombs ... Pearl Harbor!"

Japan, bombs, and Pearl Harbor. Such things and such places were far from my mind. I hardly knew a Pearl Harbor existed. Now I realized something terrifying was happening.

I was a first year student at Southwestern Baptist Seminary near Fort Worth, Texas, and was out for a Sunday afternoon stroll with a young woman friend. Up to that moment, as far as I was concerned, the only thing to get excited about was the person at my side. When it dawned on me what we'd just heard, I turned to her and exclaimed, "This means war and I'll have to go."

The world about me, both near and far, was never quite the same after that. I continued in my studies at the Seminary—I had a 4-D classification from my local draft board—but when I returned to my home in Southern California for the Christmas holidays, things were different. My brother had joined the Air Force and many of my friends were preparing to don uniforms.

I began a second year in seminary but my interest in my studies had waned, as well as my interest in the young woman. In October of 1942 I withdrew from school with the avowed purpose of entering the army. I did not know what was in store but I wanted to be where the action was. I wanted to experience military service. After the war, God willing, I would re-enter seminary.

I was about to embark upon a series of experiences unparalleled in my life. I would eventually graduate from two theological seminaries after the war, but the experiences of army life, especially combat, would also include a dynamic spiritual dimension. I wasn't certain of God's intended messages at the time, but in the ensuing years I have come to understand each one of them.

I returned to my home in La Puente, California, to ponder my decision. During this interval a friend in the ministry advised me not to go into military service but to continue in a seminary somewhere. He referred to Philippians 1:6, "Being confident of this very thing, that he which hath begun a good work in you will perform it until the day of Jesus Christ."

We talked for hours one evening, sitting in front of my fireplace. Finally I decided that military service would give me an opportunity to further seek God's will for my life.

Perhaps it might contribute something to the "good work" which He had already begun in me. It was not a cynical decision; it was the only honest thing I could do.

I signed up at a local recruiting station. I notified my local draft board in La Puente that I had given up my 4-D classification, the deferment usually granted to theological students.

On the morning of November 9, 1942, I reported to the Army Recruitment Center in the old Pacific Electric Railway station in downtown Los Angeles. My parents were with me and for a moment we stood out on the sidewalk together. I embraced my mother and then turned to shake hands with my father. As I said, "Good-bye, Dad," I saw he was crying. That was the hardest moment of all.

I don't recall that I had ever seen my father cry. He had always seemed so strong. He was about six feet tall and as a young man had played several years of minor league professional baseball. Now he was a citrus rancher. Crying, I thought, was not a part of his make-up. At that moment, however, I learned that inside that strong frame was a tender heart and mind.

Men did not often show affection for each other in those days, at least not publicly. There was a reserve in such matters and a fear that it would be interpreted as a mark of weakness. But I should have known better, that it was a natural thing in families. The Bible calls it "natural affection" or love of kindred.[1]

Often in the evening in our home my mother would read Bible stories to us, to my brother, my sister and me. My father was always close by listening. Our favorite story was that of Joseph. When Joseph revealed himself to his brothers he wept with them and kissed them all.[2] Later, when he met his father after an absence of many years, the Scriptural account says "he fell on his neck, and wept on his neck a good while."[3]

A feeling of anguish entered my heart when I saw my father crying. Standing there on the sidewalk I felt helpless and wished later that I had at least spoken a word of comfort. With only a moment of hesitation I turned and hurried into the building.

That evening about nine o'clock a bus took a group of us to Fort MacArthur near Los Angeles Harbor. Life in the

From left: Brother, Sgt. Burton Hatch; Sid Hatch, Sr.;
Sid Hatch, Jr.

army had begun. My heart was heavy but, as I reasoned, I had to be a man.

The decisions we make in life affect others. They feel the impact too. We often don't consider that. I carried the mental picture of my father's tears throughout my years in the army.

Chapter 1

How I Became a "Blackhawk"

"Though he slay me, yet will I trust in him."
—Job 13:15

"Men formerly in the ground forces must return. That's where they are needed. This is by order of General H. 'Hap' Arnold, Commanding General of the Air Force."

These in effect were the orders we received in June, 1944, at San Angelo Field, Texas. We received them almost as though they were a death sentence. We hadn't flunked anything; in fact we had hardly begun our training. Yet there they were; we read them ourselves.

Cpl. Sidney Hatch

I volunteered for military service in the fall of 1942 and received basic training at Camp Robinson, Arkansas. Most of my first year in the army was spent as a cadreman instructor, first at Camp Robinson, then at North Camp Hood, Texas. Wearying of that, I applied to the Army Air Force, took the required tests and was accepted. After a short period of time at Gulfport Field, Mississippi, our flight, as a company was called in the Air Force, was sent to San Angelo Field, Texas, for so-called "on the line" training. From there the flight was sent to a college in Oklahoma. Several of us remained behind for various reasons; for me it was three weeks in the base hospital with the mumps. We hoped to join the others later but then the fateful orders came, orders that affected us all.

An Air Force sergeant escorted a group of us via rail from San Angelo to Camp Livingston, Louisiana, near the city of Alexandria. There we were delivered to the 86th Infantry, the so-called "Blackhawk" Division, named in honor of the great Sauk Indian warrior, Black Hawk,[1] who lived from 1767 to 1838. It is from him that the Black Hawk War takes its name, a conflict in which both Abraham Lincoln and Jefferson Davis fought.[2]

We were a day late arriving at Camp Livingston. Much

Combat ready. Sid with his M.1 Garand rifle.

to our delight, we missed train connections in Monroe, Louisiana. When we finally arrived at our destination, the sergeant had some difficulty convincing the "reception committee" that our tardiness was legitimate. However, after some discussion, we became members of the 86th Division and in time, real "Blackhawks."

Two of us were assigned to Company "E" of the 342nd Infantry Regiment and I became a rifleman in the third squad of the third platoon. In a few weeks we were like family.

We trained in Louisiana and California. The time in Louisiana included maneuvers in the field, an experience which no soldier should ever forget. Our training in California included time at three different army bases, Camp Cook near Lompoc, Camp Callan near San Diego, and Camp San Luis Obispo near the city of the same name. Much of the time in California was devoted to amphibious training in cooperation with the Navy and our destination appeared to be the Pacific.[3]

During the time at Camp San Luis Obispo a wonderful event took place which, like so many experiences during my time in the military, would influence me for the rest of my life. On Saturday evening, December 9, 1944, in a church parsonage in town, Josephine Agnes Bertheau and I were married. We had met while students together at UCLA, the University of California at Los Angeles. We renewed our acquaintance during the war years, through correspondence and dates when I was home on furlough. After some persuasion on my part, and accompanied by a close friend, Jo came to San Luis Obispo and we were married.

It was a simple affair, as were so many of the soldier marriages of that time. Jo's mother and my parents and sister came up from Southern California for the occasion. Several of my army buddies were present. One of them played the piano and sang. My sister Lu was Jo's attendant and a friend from Company "K," Eugene Roddy of Philadelphia, Pennsylvania, was my best man. In the months that followed Gene would be wounded at the Danube River in Bavaria. But we are not blessed(?) with the ability to see future events, so our little wedding was a happy affair and prospects of overseas combat were submerged in the joy of the occasion.

After the wedding of Sid and Jo in San Luis Obispo, California, December 1944. From left: Eugene Roddy (wounded at Ingolstadt), Best Man; Sid; Jo; Sid's sister, Minnielu Hatch, Maid of Honor.

Jo and I honeymooned at the old Carlton Hotel in nearby Atascadero. We learned upon arrival that its dining room was closed due to the war, so we had our wedding breakfast and all our meals at a drug store counter across the street.

In the meantime events in Europe-the battle of the Bulge-changed our destination from the Pacific to the war in Europe. Within a few weeks we were on our way east to Camp Myles Standish near Boston, our port of embarkation for the European Theater.

After our marriage Jo was offered employment at a post exchange across the street from our company area at Camp San Luis Obispo. As a result, when the troop train bearing us east pulled out of the camp, she was able to stand and watch. I was able to watch her through the train window. It was a moment of agony and prayer for both of us. We could only trust the Lord for our future. Happily, I can add that these lines are being written as we begin our fifty-first year together.

About three weeks later I was walking up the gangplank of a troopship in Boston Harbor. At that moment I knew "this was it." The 86th Division was on its way to battle, the "bottom line" of warfare. It was the opposite of everything I had dreamed about in life, and now had dreamed about with Jo.

Was this a part of the "good work" which God had begun in me, or had things gone awry? Was this moment of God or of the army? Sometimes we think we have so much control of our lives, then other forces seem to enter in.

We know that God permits many things that we do not understand. He was permitting this experience and He knew the future. Nothing was to be gained by doubt or despair. As I struggled up the gangplank with my heavy overseas pack I hummed softly the words of the hymn, "Praise God from whom all blessings flow." It did help lift my spirits, for the next moment I was swallowed up by the cavernous yet crowded interior of a great troopship. The sensation of it all must have been like the moment when Jonah arrived in the belly of the whale.[4]

Chapter 2

A Voyage to Uncertainty

"They that go down to the sea...
these see the works of the LORD."
                        —Psalm 107:23-24.

We seemed to go up over a hill and then down into a valley. At least that's the way it must be described by a landlubber, for these were the hills and valleys of the sea.

To get the full effect of our experience, we often stood near the stern of the ship, rising high into the air and then suddenly sinking into a watery trough.

"They that go down to the sea in ships, that do business in great waters; these see the works of the LORD, and his wonders in the deep."[1] So wrote the Psalmist perhaps 2,700 years ago.

It was the North Atlantic in winter. We were part of a great convoy en route to Europe. The prospect of combat before us and the possibility of submarines lurking in the waters around us could not hinder the impressive might of the sea.

Eight thousand of us were traveling on the Swedish luxury liner *Kungsholm*, one of the ten largest passenger ships in the world at that time.[2] Now however it was called the *U.S.S.*

John Erickson. This former *Kungsholm* was sister ship to the diplomatic liner *Gripsholm.*

When we left Boston there were only twenty vessels in our convoy. Two days out at sea we rendezvoused with a larger convoy of forty ships, bringing the total number to over sixty, more than thirty-five of them tankers. Three combat divisions were traveling in that convoy-our own 86th Infantry, the 97th Infantry Division, and the 20th Armored Division. As a precautionary measure the entire convoy traveled in a zigzag course through the Atlantic.[3]

For a good part of the voyage one of the tankers traveled along with us to our right, or starboard. It was so laden with oil that in those heavy seas it seemed at times to go through the giant swells rather than over them. I watched fascinated as the sea water rolled over its deck.

There was time for letter writing during that long voyage across the ocean. Many of the men, I am sure, were sustained by their Christian faith, or they used it to encourage loved ones at home.

Our own officers censored the letters we wrote. One day one of them surprised us with an unusual request. "Don't refer to Bible verses by chapter and number," he said. "Write the passage out. For all we know the numbers you use could be a code, or someone could interpret them that way."

This officer's request jolted me in a way. For a moment I felt we were being denied something that was a part of our religious freedom. But as I thought about it I realized that we Christians do have a sort of cryptic way of expressing ourselves at times. From that day on, and even through combat, we never wrote such things as "Romans 8:28" or "Psalm 23:1." We quoted the passage we had in mind, regardless of its length, and omitted all the numbers. Our letters were longer but perhaps they were more meaningful, even to the censors.

One morning an announcement went round the deck, "Religious services at 1900 hours in the ship's ballroom." That evening hundreds of us crowded into the luxurious hall of that great ocean liner. Gene Roddy, my friend from "K" Company, went with me.

Hymnals were passed out and we sang, "The Way of the Cross Leads Home." It was at that moment that all the pent-up feelings of the men came out. They were not merely singing, they were praying to the God of heaven. The volume was intense and emotional. I was astonished for I had never witnessed a scene quite like it. A lump came into my throat and I felt goose flesh all over.

Two chaplains preached, simple but fervent messages that complemented each other. They were obviously moved too and the strength of their preaching fulfilled the need of

Capt. William A. Ruppar
Chaplain

the hour. One of the chaplains was Captain Gerald T. Krohn, a Presbyterian minister whose name will appear again later in this book. The other was a Lieutenant Ruppar, a Lutheran minister whose full name now escapes me.

From beginning to end, the service was forthrightly evangelistic.

Cynics may sneer and call a service at such a time "foxhole religion." That's all right. These were young men, many only eighteen years of age. They were infantrymen or members of units closely allied with the infantry in combat. They knew that in the weeks and months ahead they would be called upon to make great sacrifices and display an almost superhuman courage and endurance.

There would be periods of time when day after day they would take a sustained beating. They would need to always be alert and act instantaneously under the most adverse conditions. They would face rifle fire, artillery fire, tank fire, sniper fire, land mines, booby traps, and certain death for some of them. For days on end they would be wet, cold and tired. They would advance through mud, eat in the mud, sleep in the mud and perhaps die in the mud.[4] And they would be up against men who were enduring the same hardships, displaying the same courage and fighting on their own turf.

Can it be any wonder that on board ship that night these boys—for they were hardly more than boys—sought a little help from the Lord? The years that followed would prove that there's nothing wrong with "foxhole religion."

Experience in the infantry taught many of us how to endure the hardness,[5] not only of battle, but especially of life itself. We can let our past periods of trial guide us into a different relationship with the present moment.

As the two chaplains brought their messages to a close a moving of the Spirit of God took place in the ballroom of the *Kungsholm*—an area where revelers and party-goers had once danced lightheartedly to the strains of popular music. Gene Roddy and I were sitting to the side of that throng of men, perched high on boxes of supplies, looking out on the scene before us.

Hands went up for prayer and then moved forward to receive Christ as personal Saviour. Their hearts were hungry for some assurance for the immediate future as well as for eternity. That service and that moment remain suspended in time—the singing, the forceful preaching of the chaplains, and the unashamed looks on the faces of the soldiers. Again I was witnessing a work of the LORD, a wonder, a miracle in the deep.

Miracles do seem to come out of nowhere, but that's because God is everywhere—in the rolling billows of the sea or in a throng of teenage soldiers bound for uncertainty on the high seas. If we take the time to look around us, we'll see miracles everywhere. "Whither shall I go from thy spirit? or whither shall I flee from they presence? . . . If I take the wings of the morning, and dwell in the uttermost parts of the sea; Even there shall thy hand lead me, and thy right hand shall hold me."[6]

Chapter 3

"Bon Jour, Monsieur"

And . . . a rooster crowed."
—Matthew 26:74 (author's translation!)

We sat outside the harbor at Le Havre for two or three days before leaving the ship. The sight of the city in the distance with its spires and Old World architecture was in itself a new experience. Those men who were armed with binoculars enjoyed it to the fullest. Blown-out German pill boxes still lined the beach front.

Finally when we did disembark it was late at night and raining. We were hauled in cattle trucks about forty miles inland to a cluster of tents in a field located near the village of Ourville. This was our part of Camp Old Gold. During the days that followed I observed that nearby road signs pointed to Yvetot and Rouen.

The nights were bitterly cold there at Old Gold. No snow was on the ground but the damp air penetrated to the bone. When we crawled into our sleeping bags, it was with clothes, combat boots and all, in an attempt to keep warm, sometimes with minimal success.

Our tents were large and rectangular in shape. As I recall,

each one housed about twenty-four men. The camp was also equipped with latrines—large cavities in the earth with appropriate furniture above. A crude board wall provided a measure of privacy.

Many of the men did not want to venture out at night in the cold and darkness so they obtained large tin cans from the cook. These cans served as urinals; they were a convenience but also a hazard. One night one of my buddies, groping in the darkness for his can kicked it over. Its contents flew against the hot stove in the middle of the tent and onto some glowing red coals on the ground nearby. The results were disastrous, the smell nearly drove us out of the tent.

Despite the cold and a few other discomforts, the days at Camp Old Gold were a pleasant respite between the voyage through the North Atlantic and our introduction to combat. Little children, some wearing wooden shoes, came up to the wire fence around the camp to greet us. A young farmer with horse and plow worked the field across the road. I envied him his humdrum existence when one day I saw him eating

Camp Old Gold, Ourville, Normandy, France

his lunch—a large chunk of bread with something to drink. His life appeared to be simple and uncomplicated.

My mind went back to my home and my father's citrus ranch in Southern California. That, I now realized, had been a simple, happy and wholesome life. Sometimes we get so caught up with ambition and dreams of a career that we cannot appreciate or properly evaluate the life we have.

Ourville was within walking distance. There we could take a shower at some public baths. It was a family operated business and the pleasant proprietor accepted as payment something from our rations or supplies—half a bar of soap, or cigarettes. Those of us who did not smoke used cigarettes as "spending money."

Sergeant Eugene Bartelme and I were appointed "orientation non-coms" for the company. Bart, as we called him, was a quiet and steady fellow from Milwaukee, Wisconsin. He was one of the older men, perhaps in his upper twenties, and already a combat veteran, having served in the Aleutian campaign where he was wounded and awarded the Purple Heart. On a few occasions he shared with us the dangers and bitter cold of that campaign. Now he faced combat for the second time.

Sgt. Eugene Bartelme

Several mornings during our stay at Old Gold, Bart and I walked about two miles to another area of the camp to listen to broadcasts of the British Broadcasting Company (the BBC). There in a tent with other men we gathered round a radio to hear the latest news. Then we returned to the company and reported on the progress of the war. In these reports we tried to present as bright a picture as possible—perhaps a little news management on our part.

These long walks had certain cultural advantages too. The sight of the French farmer and his wife riding in their buggy on Friday morning, dressed nicely in dark or black clothing, told us it was market day. I don't know how much of the French language Bart knew but he told me to say, *"Bon jour, Monsieur,"* which I did and for which we received a dignified response from the couple in the buggy. I am not sure it was colloquial for that part of France, or for the occasion, but it worked.

These were days of orientation in other ways too. I remember a group of us sitting on the ground listening to an officer who had come from combat. He was explaining the organization of the German army. "And if you're captured by the S.S.," he said, "be careful. Don't try anything clever. Those guys are tough."[1]

The prospect of combat was always before us during those days in France. It was a Sunday afternoon, perhaps our last one there, when Charlie Kile approached me. "Sid, got any letters you need to write? I've got one that's pretty important. I'm going to that patch of woods up the road where things are quiet. I've got to think. Want to come along?"

Charlie explained that he was worried about things at home. He didn't want his wife to be burdened with all the business problems if he should not return. His letter was to a trusted friend and associate that he felt would take care of everything, for him and for her.

Charlie was one of the several older men in our platoon. Tall, slender and somewhat serious, he had worked for a financial institution in Muncie, Indiana, before being drafted into the army.

That Sunday afternoon is still a portrait among my memories

of World War II. It was cool that afternoon and the trees were still in their brown winter dress. Each of us sat against a tree trunk, some distance apart so we wouldn't be inclined to chat, with our rifles close at hand. In the quiet solitude we wrote our letters home—he to his trusted friend and I to Jo, my wife of only a few weeks. The letters were, as we often said then, "just in case." As we walked back to camp, we didn't say much but we felt better.

While at Old Gold we were told that non-commissioned officers also had to take a turn at guard duty. As luck would have it my turn came the first night. Mine was the last watch of the night, from about four o'clock in the morning until daylight. I walked a certain stretch of the perimeter of the camp. It was a time of quiet loneliness but also a time for reflection. It gave me an opportunity to remember how much I love this life I've been given. We forget at times that this "Gift of God" is the most precious gift of all; it's all too easy to take it for granted.

With the first glimmer of light in the east, I knew that it would soon be sunrise. In the distance a rooster crowed, confirming my observation with his shrill call. "Sounds just like an American rooster," I thought. Then the reality of where I was hit me with full force.

The Bible tells the story of a man who heard a rooster crow and, as the Scripture says, "He went out, and wept bitterly."[2] That man was the apostle Peter; he had just denied that he knew Jesus.

My reaction to a rooster crowing was not like that of Peter so long ago, but it did produce in me a moment of personal crisis—a mixture of homesickness and apprehension. I wondered if my faith would be strong enough for the experiences that certainly lie ahead. In moments like that, self-examination comes automatically.

Chapter 4

My Hohner Harmonica
(and the French "40 and 8s")

"God my maker...giveth songs in the night."
—Job 35:10

The winter cold was in the air, making the straw-covered floor of the boxcar even harder and more uncomfortable. We were crowded; a French boxcar is very small, and the only place to put our feet was to stack them in the center of the car on top of one another.

It has been a half-century since I climbed aboard a French freight train near the town of Yvetot in northern France and with other men began the slow trek toward the German lines. It's about 325 miles from that area of France to Aachen and Düren near the famous German city of Cologne and about 350 miles to the Rhine River. In wartime trains move very slowly and stop frequently. Our train rarely reached a speed of twenty miles per hour.[1]

These French freight cars were called "Forty and Eights" because their capacity was supposed to be forty men or eight horses. They were of World War I vintage and fame. Now in World War II they carried only men and their equipment with one platoon to a car—about thirty-five men.[2] These

Riding the "40 and 8s"

were our "Pullman cars" and the straw on the floor, I should add, served as the plush upon the Pullman seats.

The old boxcar was our home for two days and nights. It was very dark that first night and we were very quiet. There was no levity, no smart remarks. Except for the clatter of the rails, silence reigned.

In the bulging pocket of my fatigue uniform were some treasures from home, one of which was a Hohner "Marine Band" harmonica. I finally mustered the courage to take it out and begin to play, wondering all the time what the reaction of the other men would be.

I played small parts of several old familiar songs and then stopped. For a few moments no one said anything. Then a voice from a dark corner of the boxcar called out, "Hatch, play this song," and he mentioned a melody we all knew.

I recognized the voice. It was Sergeant Charles L. Stevenson from Washington, D.C. I was surprised. I did not know he had any interest in music or sentimental song of any kind. I played his request and then, to my surprise, he asked for another.

After that I added one or two hymns to my repertoire. I sensed that others may have been humming along with me as I played "Rock of Ages, cleft for me, Let me hide myself in Thee." Many of the fellows had been raised in religious homes.

Day and night we rode along, doing our best to make ourselves comfortable and to be cheerful. A little cynical humor was injected into the trip when one of the men in one of the other cars accidentally dropped his rifle out of the open door of the boxcar as we traveled along. Rumor had it that he would have to pay for the lost rifle, but he replied that if the army wanted him to fight it would have to give him another rifle.

We subsisted on "K" rations, which consisted of meat or cheese, hard crackers, affectionately known as "dog biscuits," dried fruit, a chocolate bar, powdered coffee, bouillon cubes, sugar and toilet paper, all packed tightly in a package about the size of a pound of butter. The menu varied a little but not much.

The railroad yards of French, Belgian, and Dutch cities became our rest stops. I especially remember Maastricht in the Netherlands, a city so prevalent in recent news stories. For us it was simply a rest stop.

It was on a Sunday afternoon, as I recall, that we were traveling slowly though the Belgian country side when we spotted a young Belgian man in civilian clothes strolling along with a female companion. Several of the men shouted at him, saying in effect, "Hey, fella, what are you doing in those civilian clothes? Why aren't you in uniform?" He and his friend only smiled in return.

There were lighter moments; a soldier learns to rise above his circumstances, and a few more times I pulled out the harmonica and dared to play. If a request came, sometimes it would be from Steve.

The train did not go all the way to Cologne. Somewhere, in an early morning darkness, we got off the train and climbed onto trucks. As daylight broke over the land we were greeted by the appalling devastation of the German city of Düren. A few miles further on we unloaded from the trucks and walked the remaining distance to Cologne. There we relieved the Eighth Division.

The next several weeks passed quickly. I carry with me now a special memory of Steve. It was during a brief fire fight in a small town. He was moving about very swiftly with a small semiautomatic weapon slung over his arm. I wasn't certain he would survive that episode, or several others, but he did. After the war ended, I did not see Steve again, but I remembered—as I do this day—his voice in the box-car.

I believe that the people who come and go through our lives must do so with a purpose. Nothing happens by accident in God's great universe, and it's up to us to discover that purpose. Each person touches our life in a distinct way. Seeing that as a gift from God can enrich our experience. And this brings me to an experience almost a half century after the war.

In 1990 my wife, Jo, and I traveled to a reunion of men from the old company. We met near White Sulphur Springs, West Virginia, at the home of Ira R. Young, one of our Company "E" buddies.[3] Dr. John F. Wood and his wife, Helen, went with us. Now a successful doctor in Oregon, John also served with us in Europe.

En route, we landed in Chicago where, thanks to bad weather, we had a long layover. While waiting in O'Hare Airport, John said, "Let's try to contact Dominic De Phillips, he was from Chicago." DePhillips was platoon sergeant for our third platoon and one of the finest non-commissioned officers in our company.

After forty-five years?" I thought. It seemed like standing in one of Chicago's busiest intersections and asking where the Smith family lived! John would not be deterred so we searched the bank of telephone directories before us but to no avail. Finally John said, "I'll try the operator."

"Can you help an old soldier from World War II find a buddy he hasn't seen in forty years" was John's approach. A helpful operator said she'd try. Shortly, she called us back with a name and a number. Astonishingly, it was the right one.

We telephoned Dominic. Our call seemed incredible to him. We talked for a while and John invited him to go on with us to the reunion. He told us, regrettably that it was impossible. Later, from our gathering in West Virginia, we talked to him and another member of our company on the telephone.

Dominic went down the list of men he remembered and with whom he had kept in touch. When he came to Steve, he said, "Sergeant Stevenson stayed in the army; he died in Korea."

The news hit hard, even after nearly half a century. I thought of just one thing, that first night in the boxcar and Steve's voice coming through the darkness asking for his favorite song.

I was a little fearful that night in the boxcar when I took out my harmonica and began to play. I know now there was a purpose in it. God gave us some songs in the night, especially a song for Steve.

The lives of two human beings touched that night in the cold boxcar. When such contacts occur we think of them as only momentary—casual, insignificant, and uninspiring. When viewed from the standpoint of eternity, the significance may be staggering. Perhaps in a brighter day and age we shall know their full impact.

Chapter 5

Our Foxhole
on the Rhine

"Behold, I will extend peace . . . like a river."
—Isaiah 66:12

Our foxhole on the Rhine River was about thirty feet from the water's edge. Despite the foxhole's location, it was deep, warm and dry, first class accommodations for two infantrymen in the front lines of combat. I shared this foxhole with one of my buddies, Staff Sergeant John L. (Johnnie) Jernigan from Waycross, Georgia.

These foxholes had been pre-pared by men of the Eighth Divi-sion whom we had relieved upon entering the city of Cologne on March 27, 1945.[1] A member of the Eighth Division, whom we chanced to meet on our arrival in Cologne, told several of our men that they had had a ter-rible time fighting their way into Cologne. German resistance had been formidable.

Our foxhole, and perhaps those

Sgt. John L. Jernigan

of others, was equipped with a telephone connecting us with men in an observation post on the street which ran parallel with the river. This was in Riehl, a part of the northern section of Cologne.[2]

Johnnie and I slipped down to our foxhole in the dark of night, making our way through a gasoline service station which, surprisingly to us bore familiar brand names such as Mobil gas and Gargoyle motor oil. We remained by the river's edge for several hours.

Those of us in the foxholes were a first line of defense should the Germans start back across the river or send a patrol in our direction. It was responsibility not to be taken lightly for opposing us on the other side were three German divisions, the 59th Infantry, the 353rd Infantry, and the 338th Wehrmacht Infantry. They were well dug in and supplied with plenty of ammunition.[3]

At the same time it was an ironic situation. We, members of a foreign invasion army, were conducting what was to the Germans almost a holy cause, a "watch on the Rhine." Witness the lines of the poet, "Dear Fatherland, no fear be thine, Firm stands thy guard along the Rhine."[4]

Once in a while the Germans would fire a flare high into the air, illuminating the entire area around us. When that happened we ducked low and played no games, such as holding our helmets above the surface of the ground. We were not interested in drawing a burst of machine gun fire or a deadly mortar shell.

Artillery boomed in the distance and not far away the massive silhouette of the great Cologne Cathedral loomed up in the night sky. It was an impressive sight, reminding us of another world, the world of spiritual values. Regardless of our religious views, we could take comfort in its looming presence. It was an assurance that the things of the

Spirit would survive the war and be waiting for us when the war was over.

There was no traffic on the river, a striking contrast to the way I would see the Rhine many years later, crowded with ships and boats, almost like a freeway. For now it was quiet and I remembered certain lines from Heinrich Heine's poem, "The Lorelei": *"Die Luft ist kühl und es dunkelt, Und ruhig flieszt der Rhein."* "The air is cool and it darkens, And calmly flows the Rhine."[5]

We had memorized the poem in my college German class and had sung it together many times. Now a few lines came back to me and while physically I remained in the foxhole, mentally I went back in time and space to a classroom in Pasadena, California. Once again I attempted to sing "The Lorelei," trying with others to sing the strange new words.

The reverie did not last long. As we scanned the surface of the water a certain amount of apprehension was unavoidable. That helped to create an almost haunting quiet in our foxhole by the Rhine (when Johnnie wasn't talking on the telephone). We could hear the swift current of the river, a sort of low roar, and the water lapping at the edge. I can still hear these sounds if I close my eyes and shut out the world around me. Having come from the arid American Southwest, everything in green, wet Germany made a deep impression on me. I had never heard or sensed the might and abundance of a great river. I knew of rivers and streams that dried up in the summer heat, but here was a stream that flowed on without end.

The prophet Isaiah speaks of "peace . . . as a river"[6] and "peace like a river."[7] Perhaps, based on his own experience in the land of Israel, he too had in mind a stream that would flow on without end. In the Messianic era there would be an abundance of never-ending peace. It is possible for us now to get a sense of that continuous flow. Isaiah also says, "Thou wilt keep him in perfect peace, whose mind is stayed on thee."[8] By opening our hearts and minds to an awareness of God's abiding presence, we can step into that flow, that river of living water.

Isaiah's beautiful word in all these passages *is shalom. Shalom* implies far more than absence of war, it includes also safety and soundness, wholeness and health.[9]

I do not want to leave the impression that all we did in Cologne was crouch down in foxholes by the Rhine. Far from it. The 86th Division was there nine days during which time there were exchanges of gunfire, mortar shells and artillery duels. We learned to duck for the nearest cover when we heard the whine of an incoming shell. There were casualties throughout the ranks of the division, and the 311th Medical Battalion established its clearing station in St. Elizabeth's Catholic Hospital in Cologne.[10]

Then there were the dreaded patrols sent across the river. They were drawn from the various companies, their purpose being to gather information and bring back prisoners for interrogation. These were dangerous missions from which some men did not return. They became "missing in action."

One day we received orders that on the following day our entire company was to go across the Rhine on patrol. It was a frightening prospect. We crowded into a large room to receive instructions from Captain Douglas C. M. Hensley from Fouke, Arkansas, our company commander.

A large map of the city of Cologne stared at us from the wall and Captain Hensley proceeded to tell us in serious tones where to go and what to do—especially if we encountered resistance, which seemed certain. Never have I listened so intently to a lecture!

Then suddenly the orders were cancelled and soon afterward we moved out of Cologne. Our relief was overwhelming. It was one of those moments when the idea of death comes closer to reality.

I have always known that the cancellation of those orders was providential and I am here today to relate this story about foxholes, rather than being part of a bloody memory on the east bank of the Rhine. Cologne

Capt. Douglas C. M. Hensley

was our "baptism of fire," our introduction to combat. And the introduction satisfied any curiosity we may have had about battle.

Chapter 6

Crosssing
the Rhine

"Thou shalt have a paddle (spade) upon thy weapon."
—Deuteronomy 23:13

On the afternoon of April 3, 1945, Company "L" of the third battalion, 342nd Infantry,[1] relieved us and we moved back from Cologne to the little town of Pesch to wait further orders.[2] These were not long in coming; in two or three days, along with the entire 86th Division, we loaded onto trucks and traveled south to Bonn where we crossed the Rhine.

It's not far from Cologne to Bonn, about 25 kilometers according to my German road map, but a military convoy moves slowly and we did not travel on any high speed highway, going rather on narrow roads through one town and city after another. As we moved through the streets of these various communities the German people generally ignored us, going about their lives with a business as usual attitude. Some of the fellows waved at the pretty German girls they saw along the way. A few of the young women smiled faintly but then quickly turned their heads away.

By now it was spring in Germany and as we traveled through the Rhine countryside the spectacle of the fruit trees in bloom made my heart sing. In some places the orchards were a sea of dazzling white and brilliantly pink blossoms. I felt uplifted, refreshed, even inspired. War or no war, the magnificent cycles of creation continued unabated. Rivers still flowed, trees bloomed, and spring brought forth its bounty.

It had been a while since I had actually taken the time to mindfully view the incredible gifts that God has bestowed upon us through nature. If only for a moment, I put war aside to take in the wonder of it all.

When we reached Bonn our convoy snaked its way slowly through a handsome residential area apparently untouched by the war.[3] Upon arrival at the river each truck moved slowly down a temporary road to the water's edge where a giant pontoon bridge awaited us, large enough to hold up the long line of heavy trucks, each one with its cargo of men. Then we began slowly to drive across the Rhine.

The river scene was beautiful. To our backs now was the city of Bonn. Ahead of us on the east bank was a beautiful forested mountain with rugged terrain apparently beyond it. Atop this high mountain was a white mansion which I was sure must be a palace.

When we were in the middle of the pontoon bridge the convoy came to a halt for no apparent reason. This left most of the trucks carrying our company sitting in the middle of the Rhine. A tour guide could not have made a better arrangement and for the moment we became tourists gazing upon the Rhineland scenery.

Suddenly the spell was broken by shouts coming from one of the trucks to our rear. Somewhat startled we all stood up to see what was happening. Was the bridge beginning to sink—or were the Germans attacking us from an unexpected quarter?

It was neither. Two trucks behind us one of the men

had stood up and was relieving himself in the Rhine River. Cheered on by his comrades, he acknowledged their shouts with a smile and a wave of his hand and proceeded to finish his business. Before it was over, he was joined by many others.

Despite the pleasant side of the journey, and even a moment or two of frivolity, it was still a hard and tiring experience. Dr. John F. Wood has described the entire trip, from Cologne to a point east of the Rhine, as "the most nerve-racking of our experience."[4]

I cannot remember now any rest stop during the entire journey. We were hurrying to take up our position on the southeast side of the so-called Ruhr Pocket. It was an encircling movement around the German forces trapped in the Ruhr industrial area.

The ablutions of the soldiers did not always coincide with the grand strategies of the generals and politicians. There were agonizing moments, especially on those long convoys, when

S/Sgt. John F. Wood

personal hygiene was important too. These young men who urinated in the Rhine did the only thing they could do; the Rhine became their latrine.

No, they were not making an obscene political statement. They were soldiers, not merchants of propaganda of which there is always an abundant supply in days of war.

Moses, when he gave instructions to the people of Israel, included the personal cleanliness of the soldier.[5] He was to carry a spade along with his weapons to cover his excrement after relieving himself. There was to be a latrine outside the camp because God moved about in the camp that He might give them victory. The camp then must be clean and the soldier himself must also be clean. A correlation existed between personal hygiene and victory on the battlefield. Jehovah, the God of Israel, could not dwell in an unclean environment.

In our experience in World War II there was a correlation between morale and personal hygiene. We tried to keep reasonably clean and we were encouraged to do so. That brief stop at the Rhine meant a lot to the soldiers. To maintain any kind of decorum under such stressful circumstances says much of their character.

In a few minutes the convoy began to move and wind its way slowly up the steep road on the other side of the river. Ahead of us lay the bitter fighting of the Ruhr Pocket campaign, a battle from which some young men in the Blackhawk Division would not return. But before that the God of grace would give our company a brief rest in a beautiful village east of the Rhine.

Chapter 7

The Village I Could Not Forget – Part 1

"For ye are all children of God by faith in Christ Jesus."
—Galatians 3:26

One evening in the late 1980s I was browsing over a road map of western Germany. I had been browsing over road maps of Germany for over forty years, always looking for a certain place but never finding it. This time turned out to be different. I had a road atlas and there at last I saw the place I had been looking for. In tiny print, close by such larger places as Breidenbach and Biedenkopf, was the little village of Wolzhausen.

The sight of the word surprised me; I had almost given up my search. Now it kindled a feeling of excitement and brought back a flood of memories.

After crossing the Rhine at Bonn we traveled east for several hours, perhaps a distance of a hundred miles, and the roads were anything but straight. Somewhere near the end of the journey the trucks carrying our company left the rest of the convoy and drove into a small village. We stopped on a side road near a rustic wooden bridge that spanned a sparkling stream.[1]

I felt a wave of deep emotion come over me as the trucks came to a halt. The village was situated in a valley between parallel ranges of low hills. The main road that went through the valley divided the town into two small residential areas, one on the east and one on the west. The side road where we stopped, with its wooden bridge over the stream, completed the idyllic scene. As my eyes swept over the landscape, I took in a deep breath, sighed, and thought to myself, "Oh, I wish we could just stay here."

We were billeted in different village homes for the night. In the morning Captain Hensley sent for Eugene Bartelme and me. "Go find the Bürgermeister and bring him here to headquarters," he said. Company headquarters, such as they were, had been set up in a brewery closed down due to the war.

Bart and I set out to find the Bürgermeister without the slightest idea where he lived. *"Wo wohnt der Bürgermeister?"* we asked in German, and some men standing near the old brewery explained that he lived across the main road on the west side of the village. We found the home easily. His wife answered our knock first and then he came to the door. We explained our mission and he came along with us quite willingly.

I have often wondered what was going through the Bürgermeister's mind as the three of us walked the half-mile back to the brewery. Even though acquiescent, Herr Bürgermeister's thoughts must have been less so. After all, he'd been rousted from his home to go meet with what he must have perceived as the enemy. That would be perturbing under the *best* of circumstances.

To make the walk a little easier for the Bürgermeister as well as for ourselves, we discussed such pertinent issues as the clouds in the sky and whether or not it would rain before sundown. It was all small talk, but I think it was comforting for the three of us. Strangely, I still remember our simultaneous glance upward and the scattered gray clouds in an otherwise blue sky.

It was a rather formal little gathering when we arrived back at company headquarters. Captain Hensley, the several lieutenants in Company "E," and Sergeant Eugene H. Walker, our company First Sergeant, were standing in a group and it fell to my lot to explain the captain's orders that the military was now the governing body of the town. Realizing the limitations of my German when it came to administrative or technical terminology, and lest I be misunderstood, I finally said, "Our captain here is now the Bürgermeister of this village." Would he convey this information to the people?

The Bürgermeister listened quietly and nodded his assent. Before the proceedings ended someone blurted out, "Ask him where the beer is." This surprised everybody, detracted from the formality of the moment, and

Sgt. Sidney A. Hatch Interpreter

perhaps embarrassed one or two. And the answer was obvious. The Bürgermeister smiled and explained jovially, as though it were new information, that due to the war the brewery was not operating and no beer was available. With this brief but lighter moment the solemn transfer of authority ended and the Bürgermeister went home.

Later, I witnessed a most amazing sight, something out of story books and centuries past. A man clad in gray trousers, a warm winter jacket and visor type cap was walking down one of the principal streets on the east side of the village. Occasionally he would pause, turn and face the houses on one side of the street, ring his bell and make an announcement. The people, leaning on their window ledges, listened.

I knew immediately he was the town crier and I assumed he was conveying to the villagers the instructions the Bürgermeister had received. I was so used to telephones and radio that this scene struck me as rather romantic, with a sense of tragedy. It couldn't have been easy for him to tell his fellow townsfolk that they had been "occupied" by invasion forces.

Earlier that first morning, even before Captain Hensley had sent for Bart and me, several of the men marched triumphantly into the house where we had slept. They were loaded down with beautiful *Federdecken,* thick, warm eiderdown quilts and blankets. They spread them out on the floor intending to use them for beds when night came. The floor of a German house is hardly a comfortable place to sleep. Someone had discovered that German homes usually have several of these comfortable and beautiful creations around.

The owners of the *federdeckes* must have had the courage to go to our officers and complain because before the morning was over an order was issued: "All *federdeckes* must be returned to their German owners."

I was one of those given this assignment and with the help of another soldier we went around loaded down with *federdeckes.* At each house the people happily identified and claimed their own. One house particularly impressed me.

We stepped inside and the people selected their blanket. In a moment my eyes swept 'round the room. Verses of Scripture, beautifully lettered and framed, adorned the walls. The family, a large group which probably included guests,[2] sat quietly, almost stoically, watching me as I stood there, rifle slung over my shoulder, reading the Scriptures.

"Am I in a Christian home?" I thought to myself. "I must be—and do I dare say anything?"

I had more blankets to return. These people were "the enemy." We were not to fraternize. I am a soldier under authority and I must obey.

But the Bible verses on the wall kindled another voice within me. Another impulse kept tugging at my heart. Two kingdoms it seemed were at war for control of my thoughts, my emotions, and my words. Little did I realize it then, but I was experiencing in that moment the power and impact of the Word of God upon the human heart and mind.

"You are a Christian," that other Voice said. "These people must also be believers." I felt so strongly the impulse to at least acknowledge the Scriptures that finally I said, speaking in German, "Those are verses from the Bible."

"Yes," the father replied, "They are selections from Holy Scripture."

A few more words were exchanged regarding the verses on the wall. I don't remember now what they were, except that it became obvious to them that I was a Christian—and I too believed the Scriptures on the wall.

During those few seconds everyone, except the father and mother, remained quietly seated around the small living room, saying nothing. The father was doing the talking, the mother standing dutifully nearby. A light soon came upon the faces of them all. Perhaps it was a mixture of delight, relief, and incredulity. Whatever it was, a new force and power, a spiritual dimension, had entered the room, and a bond stronger than war had been established.

At that moment the father turned, went to a shelf, and came back with a beautiful black leather-bound Bible in his hand. "I want to give you this," he said, "in appreciation for returning our *federdecke*." I knew it was his way of acknowledging our mutual faith in Christ.

Another soldier was with me and I realized he may have been anxious to get on with the job of returning the blankets. Also, my own internal struggle was not completely at rest and I began to feel some concern. Nevertheless, as I looked at the Bible I could not refrain from asking, "Whose Bible is this?"

"Our son's," the father replied.

"Where is your son?" I asked, and he said, "He died on the east front."

To my left on the wall was a picture of a young man in uniform. "Is that your son?" I asked, and the father answered that it was.

"I cannot accept this Bible," I said, "it's your son's. But if you have a small German New Testament and Psalms, I would like to have that."

The father turned and spoke to a young boy in the room who hurried out and came back in a moment with a New Testament in his hand. He gave it to his father who in turn presented it to me. I accepted it with thanks, then left to complete the task of returning the *federdeckes*.

No matter where we are, no matter the chaos that may be whirling around us, God can and does drop a ray of light onto our path. We can forget that wherever we are, God is there too, but He won't let us continue in forgetfulness. Whether it's manna in a wilderness or framed Scriptures on a wall, if we will but see, God is there. Thanks to the testimony of that German family, I met God again that morning. My heart was warmed and my faith was revived.

After this experience, but sometime during the same day, I received orders to come and sleep in the building next to the old brewery, just in case someone was needed to help with the German language. I found an empty upstairs room, spread my army blanket out on the floor, and there I bedded down for the several nights we remained in the village. I attempted to read the little New Testament and Psalms, although the light was dim and the floor very hard.

Before we left the village I packed the little Testament in my field pack with all my other belongings. Sometime later I rummaged through everything trying to find it, but much to my disappointment it was gone. How I lost it and where, I could not understand. A precious item became a precious memory.

Chapter 8

The Village I Could Not Forget – Part 2

"For ye are all children of God by faith in Christ Jesus."
—Galatians 3:26

Acquiescence throughout the village was complete and without incident. One morning a group of us was standing near a little stream that flowed through the village. An old man, small and frail, approached and meekly asked, *"Darf ich die Kuh melken?"* (May I milk the cow?"). I felt compassion for him, a fellow human being having to ask permission to milk his cow.

It was during our time in this village that I became engaged in a heated argument with one of the other "non-coms." It was one of the very few philosophical discussions of my time in combat, certainly the most heated, and it was a result of my contact with the German Christians whom I had met.

I was standing near the old wooden bridge when several German civilians approached me. I recognized them immediately. They were present in the living room of the home with the Scriptures on the wall at the time I returned the federdecke. They had heard my conversation with the father. As they approached me—what about I never learned—several of our own men saw them and one, a corporal, angrily shouted, "Tell those people to get the hell out of here!" I explained to the people that it was impossible to talk under the circumstances and with a puzzled look on their faces they left the area.

The corporal, accompanied by two or three other men, then approached me angrily and began to shout, "Those people don't deserve any consideration. They're all guilty and responsible for this Goddam war. You've got no business even talking to them."

With that I took issue and an angry shouting match developed between us. "All Germans did not support Hitler," I fired back. "They're not all guilty. You don't know what you're talking about."

The argument about collective guilt haunts us to this day. In wartime it's easy to see the enemy in every face—a sort of collective hatred that justifies many atrocities, often in the name of patriotism, and even religion.

I had grown up in a home of modest circumstances, yet one where political thinking was independent and able to rise above the times. My parents feared that our country was being drawn into the war in Europe. When the attack on Pearl Harbor occurred all that was set aside and we went to war, in the Pacific and also in Europe.

In 1938 I had a professor of Modern European History at Pasadena Junior College who taught us that war was sure to come in Europe because of the injustices of the Versailles Treaty, the treaty imposed on Germany at the conclusion of World War I. The seeds of the next war, he explained, are planted at the end of the preceding one. Dictators rise to power on the strength of a nation's grievances and it is the people who become their first victims.

Of far more influence on my thinking was the religious and spiritual tone of my home. My mother was an evangelical Christian and in the early 1930s—the years of the Great Depression—my father also became an evangelical.

It was a futuristic Christianity that included two principles. First, God's Covenant with the Jewish people had never been abrogated[1]—there was a national future for them—hence real Christians did not persecute the Jews and disaster would come upon a political entity that did so. Second, Christians were members of "the body of Christ."[2] This was an invisible fellowship that transcended national boundaries and made us all one in Christ. It was "the unity of the Spirit in the bond of peace."[3]

I could not therefore bring myself to actually dislike the German people. I could serve as a soldier without a heart filled with hate. Because I sympathized with the plight of the Jews and recognized the evil purpose behind their suffering, did I automatically have to hate another ethnic group, an entire nation of individuals? No, that was inconsistent with the message of Christ. There could be, even in Nazi Germany, Christian people of the same spirit, people with insight into the times,[4] and I knew I had met some of them in the little village.

Motivated, albeit unconsciously, by these ideals, I nonetheless allowed myself to become incensed at the corporal's words. I was dealing with someone who refused to rise above the immediate circumstances of combat and who wanted to drag me down with him.

As the discussion became more heated, other men began to gather around. One of the lieutenants, hearing the ruckus, walked over to see what was going on. He listened for a moment and then said, "Okay, men, let's break it up. Corporal Smith (not his real name), move on."

In a moment the lieutenant and I were the only ones standing by the bridge. I wondered what he would have to say to me. Perhaps something about "fraternization," I was a little nervous.

"You know, Hatch," the lieutenant began, "I'm sure looking forward to the day when this war is over. My dream is to get back home to South Dakota, get the ol' fishing rod out, and park by a stream somewhere." We both stood there for a moment, leaning on the rail of the bridge.

"Yes, sir," I said, "my thoughts are along the same line. "I'll have to admit, I've got a lot of dreams and hopes too. It'll be a great day when the war is over and we all go home."

We remained in that village for several days altogether. It was a pleasant respite for us while the war raged elsewhere in Europe. Someone remarked, "We may sit out the war right here in this village." Such wishful thinking betrayed the secret prayer in the heart of more than one fearful G.I. But such was not to be.

The day came when we had to leave. The campaigns in the Ruhr and then Bavaria still lay ahead of us. We gathered near the wooden bridge that crossed the stream to await the convoy of trucks that would take us away. In a few minutes it arrived and the fellows began to climb aboard.

I glanced toward one of the village streets and coming down the slope toward us were some of the civilians. I recognized them again as having been among the group that was in the house with the Bible verses on the wall. They were approaching me. Perhaps, I thought, they only wished to say goodbye.

An officer standing nearby shouted, "Tell the people to get back!" I raised my arm and they stopped about twenty feet away. I conveyed my orders; we could not converse. Then I reminded them of the second coming of Christ and, as best I could in German, referred to a few of the phrases in I Thessalonians 4:13-18, "I'll see you then," I said. That was my final word. The expressions on their faces let me know that, although somewhat perplexed by the circumstances of the moment, they understood what they had to do. The lieutenant, a different one this time, did not say anything.

We sat in the trucks waiting to pull out. Bart, my companion on the long walks in France and the sergeant who had gone with me to find the Bürgermeister, remarked most casually, "The name of this village is Wolzhausen." I thought to myself, "I must remember."

For more than forty years I wondered if I had heard Bart correctly and if there really was a Wolzhausen. Thanks to my college German class, I assumed it was spelled, *Wolzhausen*. But I could never find it on maps of Germany and no one I spoke to seemed to know of such a place.

The names of most of the towns and villages have been forgotten, if I even knew them in the first place, but not that of Wolzhausen. The events there taught me much spiritual truth. We experience two kingdoms in this universe of ours. One is "the kingdom of the world," the other is the kingdom "of our Lord and of his Christ."[5] The first seems real, but is, in fact, temporary. It can grip our minds. The second kingdom has a grip upon our hearts, more than we realize. We often bring the two kingdoms into conflict with each other by letting the temporary lull and deceive us into a false sense of control and security. We truly belong to the second and permanent kingdom and are, as Paul says, "the children of God by faith in Christ Jesus."[6]

For over forty years I felt that, most likely, I would never know the name of the German family in the house with the Scriptures on the wall. I did not think to ask and they did not tell me. After all, we were not supposed to fraternize.

We often forget, as William Cowper wrote, that God moves in a mysterious way His wonders to perform.[7] In 1990 I did learn the name of the family whose home was blessed with the Scriptures on the wall. Even the name of the humble old man who asked permission to milk his cow! That story I shall tell before the conclusion of this book.

Part II

In the Ruhr

Chapter 9

Some Background for Blessings in Hell

(Introduction to Ruhr Pocket Fighting)

"War is hell."[1]
—William Tecumseh Sherman, 1879
"Out of the belly of hell cried I, and thou heardest me."

—Jonah 2:2

On April 8, 1945, our pleasant interlude in Wolzhausen came to an end. We loaded onto the trucks and headed into the fighting in the Ruhr industrial area of Germany.[2] Word had come from our 342nd regimental command post at nearby Ober Dieten that it was time to enter the fray.

The fighting in the Ruhr came to be known as the Battle of the Ruhr Pocket. This so-called pocket was created when the U.S. Ninth Army troops in the north met U.S. First Army troops coming up from the south at the German city of Lippstadt about one hundred miles northeast of Cologne. This juncture of the two armies took place during the last week of March. As a result, about 325,000 German troops became encircled.[3]

At this point General Dwight Eisenhower had to make a momentous decision. Should he simply "contain" the Wehrmacht units trapped in the Ruhr while the main body of his armies raced eastward to capture Berlin? Or should he draw up to the Elbe River and wait there while the German army in the Ruhr was attacked and destroyed? This latter course would eliminate any possibility that the surrounded German forces might break out of the Ruhr Pocket and disrupt his lines of communication to the east.[4]

Eisenhower decided upon the latter policy—to eliminate the Ruhr Pocket first. As we know now, this was a fateful decision. It affected the course of events in the east and in Berlin. For Company "E," and for this writer, it meant a series of intense combat experiences.

The Battle of the Ruhr Pocket was not a case of two gigantic armies meeting head-on, as North and South met at Gettysburg, and the issue being decided in a day or even several days. As the American forces closed in from the north, east and south it became a series of deadly skirmishes. For more than a week we did not stop moving, maneuvering and fighting. It seemed much longer!

We can probably all look back at dark points in our lives, points that seemed interminable; yet we emerged from them. We are not always left with the most pleasant of memories. We can, however, choose to view these memories from a different perspective. God's light can shine in the darkness of memory, as well as in any other area of our lives.

The Ruhr had been heavily defended against Allied air attacks by anti-aircraft batteries or "flak guns." As we moved through the forests I observed that the trees were covered by metallic-like material which reminded me of the tinsel on Christmas trees. It had been dropped by our Air Force in an effort to thwart the effectiveness of their radar.

Richard A. Briggs, who was at the time an eighteen year old rifleman in Company "I" of the 342nd Infantry, has written that a flak gun was located at nearly every village, hamlet and crossroad in the Ruhr. When the ground forces approached, these flak guns were lowered and fired point blank into our combat troops.[5]

It was the mission of the 342nd to drive north through the hills and valleys in the southern sector of German's Ruhr industrial area. The city of Hohenlimburg, located on the Lenne River near the larger city of Hagen, was about sixty miles away (as the crow flies), and was our ultimate objective.

The drive north was no easy task. Not only were we confronted by formidable defenses and courageous defenders, we also had to overcome difficult terrain, steep mountains and hills, narrow valleys, and dense forests. In many instances our only access through the terrain was a dirt road or fire break. Combine all that with dark and sleepless nights. Much of the time we were cold, wet, exhausted and afraid. There was the never ending fear of snipers as we moved, sometimes clumsily, through the trees and forests. On one occasion, as our company rounded the bend on a narrow dirt trail in the mountains, machine gunners, snipers, and flak gunners suddenly opened fire on the men in the lead. Seven of them were instantly cut down, one of whom, PFC. Thomas A. Hastie, died of his wounds four days later.[6] Briggs, in his history of the 86th, has expressed it well: "Throughout the Ruhr there was agony, and there was not glory in it except the glory of courageous men–men of the Black Hawk Division."[7]

During this period in the Ruhr, I, too, witnessed the resolve and dedication of my compatriots. To continue under such barrages without cracking is a testimony to courage, strength and sense of purpose. I got a peek into the human character not afforded to many people and which does not come often in life. The memory of this continues to challenge and inspire me in the cloudy and dark days of my life.[8]

It is against this background that God allowed me to begin having a series of experiences that will be related in following chapters. It is not my purpose here to attempt a detailed description of the Ruhr campaign, or even our small part in it. That is far beyond the narrow scope of this work. I have related only those experiences which have had a major spiritual impact upon my life. Their value continues to increase; after fifty years I am still deeply affected by them.

America's famous Civil War general, William Tecumseh Sherman, once said, "War is cruel and you cannot refine it." On another occasion he uttered his even more famous words, "I am tired and sick of war. Its glory is all moonshine. It is only those who have neither fired a shot nor heard the shrieks and groans of the wounded who cry aloud for blood, more vengeance, more desolation. War is hell."

Sherman was right. War is hell and we cannot refine it. It is better to admit that, to make war appear as it actually is. We can begin by deglorifying it, making it appear less noble and righteous. But, even in hell—maybe especially there—God can bestow a blessing.

Chapter 10

Jim's Courage

(and His Brown New Testament)

"Come ... O breath, and breathe upon
these slain, that they may live."
—Ezekiel 37:9.
"Jesus said ... I am the resurrection, and
the life: he that believeth in me, though he
were dead, yet shall he live."
—John 11:25

We looked down at Jim. He was unconscious and breathing heavily. A bullet had entered his face under his left eye.

As we stood there on the street of the German town of Hofolpe gazing helplessly at a severely wounded buddy, my mind flashed back in time to Camp San Luis Obispo, California. We were engaged in amphibious landing training, preparatory to fighting in the Pacific.

I hurried into Jim's quarters one evening to ask if he was going to town and to the service center. "No," he replied, "I'm not going. I've been kind of 'down' lately and have started reading the New Testament. I'll stay here and read."

Jim was sitting on the edge of his bunk, an open New Testament in his hand, one of those small brown ones the chaplains used to give to soldiers. His response was a surprise and made a strange impression on me. I made no effort to dissuade him from his decision and went on my way. As I left the barracks I felt warmed in spirit because I hadn't been aware of Jim's interest in the Bible.

A few months later, because of the course of events in Europe, we were on a troop train together, headed for a port of embarkation on the east coast rather than the west coast. Our route of travel took us near Jim's home in Kansas City, Missouri. He could see "the old neighborhood" in the distance. A powerful impulse, he told us later, made him feel like leaping from the train and going home. No one would have blamed him. We were already homesick ourselves.

It did not take long to get us into combat: port of embarkation at Boston, arrival at Le Havre, orientation in France and then up to the German lines at Cologne.

Now, about a week after leaving Cologne, our experience in the Ruhr Pocket fighting was just getting under way. One afternoon two platoons of our company, the second and third, rushed down a wooded mountain side into Hofolpe hoping that our arrival would be a complete surprise. As it turned out, a number of German soldiers were there to welcome us and a battle ensued.

Some members of our platoon were pinned down by hostile fire coming at them from the second story of a nearby house. Jim volunteered to try to get to high ground behind the house. In doing so he could at least divert the attention of those firing at our men. As he moved into the open he exposed himself to their fire and was shot.

The fighting soon ended. Several of us gathered round Jim during those last few moments of his life. An officer from the medical corps came up, knelt beside him, and placed a small metal mirror under his nostrils. I noticed as Jim exhaled that the mirror would fog up. The time between each breath became longer, then it stopped. When there was no condensation upon the mirror we knew that his breath of life was gone. The officer spoke quietly, "He's dead."

We tarried a few seconds, then had to turn and walk away, leaving Jim lying in the street. It seemed as though we were abandoning him. Who would retrieve him after we left? I thought about his parents and family at home. Would his dog tags be all they had left of him? I prayed secretly that somehow his body would find its way home.

Quickly, though, I let Jim slip from my mind—for the moment, at least. More of us would be shot, more of us would die. To dwell too long on the loss of one, well, it was a luxury I couldn't afford.

In 1975, while engaged in a pastorate at Wallingford, Connecticut, my wife, Jo, and I read about a church conference in nearby Hartford. We decided to attend one of its sessions, thinking we might see some friends from the west coast. Also, I knew that one of my friends from Company "E" days, Pfc. Phil C. McLain, had entered the ministry after the war and was serving a pastorate in that particular denomination.[1] Perhaps he would be there.

Much to our delight, Phil was present at the conference. During our brief reunion, we reminisced about our days in the army and time in combat. Jim's name then entered the conversation. Phil had been a jeep driver for our company; he said he came and got Jim that afternoon in Hofolpe, lifted him into his jeep and carried him with him during the evening hours until it could be ascertained where Jim was to be taken. I felt a wave of relief.

Pfc. Phil C. McLain

In June, 1993, a letter from a Dutch reader in the Netherlands appeared in the *Blackhawk Bugle*, the official paper of our 86th Blackhawk Division Association.[2] Accompanying this letter was a list of names of 86th Division men buried at Margraten in the Netherlands. It included two names from our company: James N. Curtis, Jr., and Thomas A. Hastie. The dates beside their names were April 10, 1945, and April 11, 1945. It was good to know, after all these years, where both men were resting. My secret prayer had been answered.

God knows the day of our birth and the day of our death. In His foreknowledge He knew that Jim would die on April 10, 1945. He could have intervened to stop it and Jim's life would have been spared. But He did not do that. I do not know why—"who hath known the mind of the Lord?"[3] But in His mercy He prompted Jim to stay "at home" in the barracks that evening in San Luis Obispo and read his New Testament. And if God went that far, He must have guided Jim to certain verses and opened his heart to their message.

Pfc. James N. Curtis, Jr.

For his valor Jim received the Silver Star. I know we'll see each other again, not because of the Silver Star but because of the promises in his little brown book. I do not know what passages of Scripture he was reading that evening in San Luis Obispo. I do know that, whatever they were, he was reading words of life.

Jesus has said, "I am the resurrection, and the life; he that believeth in me, though he were dead, yet shall he live."[4] Jesus, God's son, is the worker of resurrection and the giver of resurrection life.[5] The person who believes in Him, even if he should die, will live again in the resurrection of the dead. This is a certainty for Jim and for all who trust in God's Son.

Chapter 11

"Du Bist Wie Eine Mutter"

("You Are Like a Mother")

"If thine enemy hunger, feed him; if he thirst, give him drink."
—Romans 12:20

As dusk settled over Hofolpe our platoon was directed to a nearby house. We'd spend a few hours there, perhaps the night, before moving on.

The afternoon had been intense and severe. Jim Curtis had been killed and the German casualties lie grotesquely in the street a few yards away.

The prisoners had been rounded up and searched before being led away. Someone in the meantime had located the Bürgermeister, and Captain Hensley demanded of him to be shown a room where he could set up company headquarters. This was one of those occasions when I was ordered to come along and interpret.

As we walked along, the Bürgermeister asked if the Captain would like a glass of wine but he declined in no uncertain terms. He did not need to be mollified. The Bürgermeister then asked if he could do something about *die Kameraden* lying in the street. Clearly it was his intent that they should be picked up for burial or returned to their families. When

I conveyed this request to the Captain he replied brusquely in the negative. To the Bürgermeister, however, I softened the reply.

For a moment I felt sick at heart. The Captain had a point; there are priorities in war that don't exist at other times. But to tell the Bürgermeister that his dead comrades could continue to lie in the street went against every instinct in me.

It bothered me to walk away from Jim Curtis; it bothered me to consign the same fate, if only temporary, to the German dead. Death, it seemed to me, canceled out hostility. We were no longer dealing with friend or foe; we were dealing with human beings in the image of God. To honor the dead, I realized then, was not a trite principle.

I did not reveal my feelings. In a little while a suitable house and room were located and the Bürgermeister went his way and I went back to my platoon.

When I arrived at the house I joined the other fellows in eating some of our "K" rations and trying to get organized for the night. I happened to see myself in a mirror and my face was flushed and red from the events of the afternoon.

Ironically—or perhaps providentially—our third squad was told to sleep on the floor of the living room while the other men went upstairs. Across the hall was the kitchen and in the hallway, just inside the front door, was a small vestibule area. There in the hallway, not far from the front door, lay a wounded German soldier. How he got there or who brought him in I did not know. We had to walk by him each time we left the room, and I must admit, at first I tried to ignore him.

When it grew dark we lay on the floor and tried to sleep. But sleep was not coming easily to any of us. I was doing a lot of thinking; now I knew what it was like to be in aggressive close combat, to see men get shot and to watch them die. Something else re-entered my mind. I began to think about the wounded German lying on the floor not far away. Why hadn't he been taken away with the other prisoners, and who had carried him into "our house"? Then a disturbing thought began to prey upon my mind: perhaps I should go help him—but what would the other fellows think?

Finally I could stand it no longer. I rose from my makeshift bed on the floor and feigned an excuse to leave the room. In the hall I stood and looked down at the man on the floor. I could hear him trembling and his teeth chattering.

Returning to the living room, I said to Johnnie Jernigan, our squad leader, "Johnnie, the wounded German out there is trembling and chattering. Maybe we ought to help him."

To my pleasant surprise, Johnnie was concerned too, so the two of us went out into the hallway and knelt down beside the German. Hardly had we done so when two other fellows from our squad came and knelt down with us. None of us were medics; at the moment we had no idea what we could do, but I think we all wanted to do something. Something was better than nothing.

The German soldier looked up at us. Miserable as he may have been, he was still aware of the activity around him. I ventured then to ask a few questions.

Where was he wounded? Shrapnel had gone through his right thigh and imbedded itself in his left leg. When did it happen? Out on the mountain side that afternoon.

His feet hurt. They were swollen inside his large black army boots. The two fellows who had come to help us worked together and removed them. With that the German soldier heaved a great sigh of relief. I observed that his feet were clothed in heavy gray woolen socks and their thickness obviously added to his discomfort.

He was miserable in other ways too and we suspected

what it was. I did not remember the German phrases for the ablutions of the inner man but that was not necessary. I resorted to the universal language of onomatopoeia and he understood perfectly.

"Get a bowl from the kitchen," I said to the two fellows who were helping us, "that will serve as a urinal." While Johnnie and I propped him up he relieved himself into the bowl. Again he almost groaned in relief and handed the bowl to our two helpers. "What'll we do with it?" they asked. "Pour it down the sink," I replied.

Perhaps some hot bouillon, the kind that came in our "K" rations, would taste good to him. I asked if he would like some *Suppe* and this brought an enthusiastic and affirmative response. One of our men volunteered to warm a canteen over some canned heat.

The German soldier's main problem was his wounds. Something had to be done to relieve his suffering. I thought of Pat Gallagher,[2] our medic. He was upstairs, so one of the men went and got him. A shot in the arm was Pat's suggestion.

I asked our patient about *das Morphium* and he gave his consent. So we rolled up his sleeve and Pat injected into his arm the contents of a tube smaller than a free sample of toothpaste.

Now the bouillon was ready. Kneeling beside him, we held him up again while he drank it with relish and satisfaction. Then blankets were brought and carefully tucked around him so that he might be warm throughout the night. A pillow was rigged up for his head and assurance given that soon he would be asleep and relieved of his suffering.

"There is not much more we can do," I said to him, and I was sure we would soon be on our way. Perhaps, I consoled him, he would be found in the morning. Maybe even taken to an American hospital. Then it was possible the war would soon be over and he would return home to his family.

He looked up, a smile flickered across his face and he said, *"Du bist wie eine Mutter."* "You are like a mother." We both laughed but his words pierced my heart.

When our ministrations were done and our patient was settled for the night we went back into the living room and lay down on the floor. Nobody said anything, we were all deep in thought.

About 3:30 in the morning we were awakened and told to get ready to move out. Again we had to step over and around the wounded German but now we observed with satisfaction that he was sleeping soundly.

In the cold darkness of the early morning we stood out front in the street waiting for the trucks to come take us away. "Did you notice how the German was sleeping?" someone asked. "Yeah, just like a baby," a voice chuckled in reply.

At that moment the trucks arrived. We climbed up into the back of the army truck and headed out—we knew not where—for another day at war. The street of Hofolpe was empty now. Jim Curtis was gone, someone had come and picked him up, and the German casualties were gone too. Their own people, I presumed, had come and taken them away.

It was the morning of April 11, 1945, the day our company would be ambushed on the mountain road and Thomas Hastie would receive his mortal wounds. But a kind God does not let us see into the future, not even a day at a time.

There is a place within each of us, a place of sympathy and nurture, that often shows itself when a fellow human being is in distress. This desire to care for another can even override orders and authority. We truly touch each other in these moments. When these times become more frequent, war begins to appear meaningless.

Epilogue

I often think of my German friend; in my memory he has become a friend. What was his name? Did he recover? Is he alive somewhere in Germany today? I wish I knew. We had a brief encounter in time and space. We touched hearts. Even in the midst of war and death, the light of Christ shown—through the compassion of human beings.

Perhaps someday I shall know the answers to these questions, and many more. Perhaps they are known in Hofolpe today.

War is what General Sherman said it was. And there are higher principles that can salvage our experiences and transform them. Jesus said, "Blessed are the merciful: for they shall obtain mercy."[3] Therefore Paul wrote, "If thine enemy hunger, feed him: if he thirst, give him drink."[4]

Chapter 12

Hands Upon Shoulders in the Darkness

(and a Mission of Mercy in the Morning)

*"Thou hast beset me behind and before,
and laid thine hand upon me."*

—Psalm 139:5

The darkness that night seemed to cover us and wrap around us. There were many dark nights in Germany in 1945, and this one was the darkest of all.

I do not know exactly where we were except that it was one of the towns in the Ruhr. This experience fits somewhere into our Ruhr Pocket chronology and it must have been a day or two—or a night or two—after our experience in Hofolpe. The memory of the experience is vivid. The memory of the dates and place have faded.

Our objective was to get to the top of a steep hill located in the environs of the city and to hold that position until daylight. One side of the hill had a steep ascent, the other ended in a precipitous bluff overlooking part of the suburbs. It was covered with trees and its topography and location gave it much in the way of strategic value. Captain Hensley and the men who were leading the company had located the path which led to the summit and that was the way we were to go.

As we stood at the base of the hill waiting for orders to move, the message came down the line, "Sling your rifles. Move out single file. Put your hand on the shoulder of the man in front of you. Don't turn loose of him. Don't go to the left or right, you might slip off the path."

Thus it was that we began our ascent to the top, in a darkness so thick we could not see the ground and with the possibility of being greeted by gunfire anywhere along the way. One hundred and fifty men or more, virtually blind, moved single file up the steep, narrow trail.

A man's hand was resting upon my shoulder and my hand was resting upon that of the man in front of me. It was an unusual sense of responsibility as we groped our way upward. I realized that I must hold on, not merely for my sake but for the sake of a hundred men behind me. I did not want to be the weak link in the chain. If it should be broken and our company became divided and confused, the results could be disastrous.

In later years I read some verses in the "Book of Psalms" that reminded me of that night in Germany. "Thou hast beset me behind and before, and laid thine hand upon me . . . If I say, Surely the darkness shall cover me; even the night shall be light about me."[1]

The darkness may seem to "cover" us, even "fall upon" or "overwhelm" us.[2] But before and behind is the presence of God. He lays His hand upon us.

Such was our experience at the moment. We felt almost immobilized and overwhelmed by the darkness but we experienced a deep bonding. I experienced an almost desperate need to hold on to the man in front of me, and an equal fear of stumbling off the path. I felt the grip upon my shoulder of the man behind me. Living through that moment, I am sure, changed us all, though our thoughts at the time were strictly of survival.

The chain was not broken and we reached the top of the hill. The ground was hard and rocky making it virtually impossible for us to dig foxholes or any kind of entrenchment. At the same time a drizzling rain kept falling so, in an effort to keep warm, we huddled together under our raincoats and waited for the dawn.

The shells of the artillery whistled over our heads all night. All I could think was, "I hope none of them fall short." While in training at San Luis Obispo, California, one of our men had been killed by a mortar shell that fell short. A few days later four of our fellows were injured by shrapnel and flying rocks from supporting fire from one of the other companies. Such is the irony and tragedy of so-called friendly fire. Mistakes can be deadly. But this was no mistake. It might end for us all with one hit. I knew it. We all knew it. We weren't laughing.

When daylight came we could see where we were. Down the path we had ascended was a small building. We had passed it in the night without realizing it was there. A few of us decided to venture down and see what it contained. It turned out to be a small mountain lodge.

We entered the door facing the path and found ourselves in a tiny kitchen and dining area. Some German civilians were there, several women and a man. They had taken refuge there during the attack upon the city. These were middle-aged people and all quite conservatively dressed. I carry with me to this day a mental picture of the man, for he was wearing gray slacks, a black coat, and shirt and tie. We hadn't seen a civilian gentleman dressed that way for a long time. It was obvious that the stress of war, even the battle at hand had not forced him to compromise his personal dress code. The only thing lacking in his apparel was a brief case.

The civilians had probably heard us passing in the night, groping our way up the path. One can only imagine what went through their minds at the time. They eyed us cautiously and we pretended to ignore them. They had been attempting to prepare some sort of breakfast for themselves and we set about to do the same—something from our "K" rations, especially coffee. We noticed with appreciation that they had gotten a fire started in the wood burning stove so the fellows gave it a boost with a few sticks of kindling.

It was at this point that the barriers broke down, prompted by our mutual desire for warmth and a hot drink in the morning. They were preparing what we assumed to be their ersatz coffee or substitute product so we offered them some of the coffee from our rations, even if it was in powdered form. They readily accepted.

The man in the group pulled a picture post card out of his inside coat pocket and showed it to me. He had received it from a friend or relative in America, and perhaps had saved it for such a moment as this—an encounter with the Americans. I recognized the picture immediately. It was the famous Rainbow Pier at Long Beach, California. I told him I had been swimming there many times.

One of the women in the group explained to us that if she could go down the hill to her home she would retrieve some food for all of them, especially a jar of fruit. But she was afraid to go alone, would some of us go with her? It was risky business for us too but we wanted to help. Finally, with the assent of the other men, two of us decided to go.

The street was in a shambles, broken glass was everywhere and it was not hard to see why she hesitated to go alone. As the three of us walked along, the woman always walking between us, some unpleasant looking individuals wandering through the rubble glowered at us, and especially at the German woman. I had the feeling that they resented what we were doing. I was also impressed by their appearance that they were not a part of the local German population, perhaps foreign workers or displaced persons who were now free to move about as they pleased. Whoever they were, they made us feel very uncomfortable and I was glad we had our rifles.

The German woman retrieved a jar of fruit from her cellar along with some other items from the house and at our urging we hurried back to the lodge on the hill. We were never certain what might be waiting for us around each corner, behind the bombed-out rubble. There could have been snipers, or even that final hold-out ready to throw his last grenade. I'm still amazed at the risk we took for a jar of fruit.

Fortunately the company was still on the hill and the men were waiting for us in the lodge. We ended that mission of mercy none too soon.

Such are the contradictions and paradoxes of war. I remember the night and its darkness but I cannot separate it from the morning after. It is easy for us sometimes to blend memories, to overlap them, even to construct them out of thin air. We do it for protection, for survival, or perhaps convenience. For those of us on that hill, the bonding we experienced will remain a clear memory. For many, and particularly for me, it was literally the darkest night of the war.

During my years in the Christian ministry I have preached many times from Psalm 139. When I come to the verses quoted above, I think of that night in the Ruhr. The Psalmist too had some great experiences in the darkness, even ones of danger, that helped him to realize the presence of God all about him.

Retrieving some food from the woman's shattered home

in town was a harrowing experience, but I have no regrets. It was a small gesture which, thankfully, proved successful. I know we all felt good about sharing our coffee with the civilians in the lodge. We were hoping the world would be a better place after the war.

Chapter 13

The Slaughter of the Cooks

"Shimei ... came forth and cursed (David)."
—II Samuel 16:5-6
"And David said ... let him alone, and let him curse; for the LORD hath bidden him."
—II Samuel 16:11

"Every man get in the ditch alongside the road. If they come through our ranks, each man pick a man!" These were our orders as we awaited the column of German troops coming toward us on the road.

The men in battalion headquarters had been hauling our rations to us when they drove into an ambush. The trucks were riddled with enemy fire, two of the drivers were killed, and several men were captured. One of our men, Wallace R. Stasielowski from Massachusetts,[1] escaped death by piling ration boxes around himself in the truck.

We did not eat that day and at nightfall we started out to recover our men and our rations. It was the beginning of a night that I am sure is etched on all of our memories. It came near the close of our Ruhr Pocket fighting.

As we advanced, the captain and the scouts up ahead heard oncoming troops and horse drawn vehicles. In a moment we could all hear them: the noise of the wagon wheels, the clop clop of the horses' hoofs, the voices of the German troops, and in the final seconds their shadowy figures approaching us. We waited in the ditch with rifles ready and fingers on the trigger. Not one of our men stirred or made a sound.

Were we afraid or scared? I am sure most of us experienced a certain amount of fear and apprehension, yet I can honestly say that in those final seconds another feeling prevailed over fear: it was a determination not to get killed—to fire one's rifle first—and that, I would guess, was the feeling of most of us. We had been trained for such moments as this.

When the first horse drawn vehicle became even with the beginning of our line of men, Captain Hensley resorted to an act of raw and reckless courage. He leaped out of the ditch, took the lead horse by the bridle, and gave the order to fire.[2] The night air was ripped apart by the noise of the rifles and the cries of the German soldiers hit by the rifle fire. Their consternation was visible to us, even in the darkness. The soldier in the lead suddenly and wildly threw himself to his left as he was hit by the first blast of the rifles.

It was all over in a few seconds. The German column never reached our positions in the ditch, about forty or fifty feet down the line. If there were any men behind their leaders, they escaped in the darkness.

"Let's go," the voices up ahead shouted and we climbed out of the ditch and moved forward. The wounded men lay groaning upon the ground as we walked on by them. It pained us deeply but we had no choice. The lead horse, with head lowered as though in grief, stood quiet and motionless in his harness as we passed by.

The wagon which the horse had been pulling contained

a huge cauldron filled with beef stew. We looked at it and smelled it, its fragrance filling our nostrils. "Don't touch it," someone shouted and we kept moving ahead.

Then something totally unexpected happened. There were several houses nearby and the rifle fire brought some of the people out of their homes. A number of them had gathered in the yard just across the ditch from where I was at the moment. Suddenly a woman, then a man, moved forward and began to shout at us.

I looked at this woman, now only a few feet away. She was very tall and she seemed to hurl her reproaches right at me. I didn't understand her words—they were new to me—but I didn't need to. Her message was clear. The picture and the sound of her voice, totally without fear, rallying to the defense of her country and the men on the ground, is still vivid in my mind. The man who came forward with her stood to her right and back a short distance. He yelled a little but she was the one who truly conveyed their anger and agony.

No one at the head of our column heard these people. And not a man in our ranks said a word in response. I just wanted to keep moving. I think everybody felt the same way. As a company we did what war required us to do. At the moment it seemed to be the only way. As for the people, we felt their anguish. Let them curse us. Our mouths were closed by the circumstances, even as our hearts remained open.

The Bible tells of a man named Shimei who cursed King David when the latter was fleeing from his son Absalom. As the king and his entourage came to Bahurim, a village northeast of Jerusalem, Shimei cursed David, threw stones at him, and called him a "bloody man" or "man of blood."

Abishai, one of David's men, wanted to go over and take off Shimei's head. David demurred, "Let him curse, because the LORD hath said unto him, Curse David."[3]

The message in that story is a little clearer because of what happened that night in Germany.

In ancient Israel, following the death of King Saul, there was a long war between David and the house of Saul. It was a war which entailed much bloodshed, but in the process, the Scripture says, David became stronger and stronger while the house of Saul became weaker and weaker.[4]

Shimei was from the tribe of Benjamin and the house of Saul. When he saw David in flight from Absalom, his long-simmering loyalty to Saul exploded in curses toward David. David understood and in a way of thinking perhaps strange to us, saw in the incident the hand of God. It reminded him of many things in his past, even of the fact that his own son Absalom had gone to war against him.[5]

God let the German woman and the others with her shout at us that night. No doubt she expressed the pent-up feelings of many of her people. More importantly, it was a way of reminding us of the terrible business we were in. Later, however, during our time in Germany, the surprising and courageous demand of a German pastor would remind me that God uses all circumstances in His plan to establish peace on the earth. There'll be more on that later.

We do not immediately see the purpose or lesson in an event, no matter how terrible it is, nor can we judge it altogether by its outward appearances. Many times in Scripture we are admonished not to judge by appearances.[6]

As we heard the oncoming German troops, the grinding sound of the wagon wheels, the clop clop of the horses' hoofs, and the voices of their men in the lead we did not know the character of their force or the strength of their numbers. In such a predicament and with the lives of a hundred and fifty or more men in his hands, Captain Hensley had to make a quick and terrible decision. He could do no other.

Very often, those standing outside a situation are the first to condemn those within it. They fail to grasp the whole picture. They become self-righteous. We all have been guilty of that reaction at one time or another; as Paul says, "all have sinned, and come short of the glory of God."[7]

Rations reached us in the morning and we found Wallace Stasielowski, our man who had been captured. He and others were being held in the lower area of a German *Gasthaus*. "How did they treat you?" I asked him a day or two later. "All right," he replied very quietly.

Chapter 14

"I Will to Go Home"
(The God-given Instinct)

*"Foxes have holes, and birds of
the air have nests."*
—Luke 9:58.

*"Be it ever so humble, there's no
place like home."*[1]
—John Howard Payne (1792-1852)

It was early in the afternoon of Sunday, April 15, 1945. The Battle of the Ruhr Pocket was in its last stages. Our regiment, the 342nd Infantry, was nearing its objective, the industrial city of Hohenlimburg on the Lenne River.

Company "E" approached Hohenlimburg on a narrow dirt road leading down from a hill into the city. A small band of German soldiers, perhaps a dozen men, came up the road to meet us. Their only desire was to surrender; for them that would be the end of the war.

As far as soldiers go, these were older men, certainly men in middle age. Included in their ranks was a lad of about fifteen. As we stood there in a group, Germans and Americans, this lad began to exclaim, "I will to go home! I will to go home!" His English was influenced by his mother tongue. He was probably thinking, *"Ich will nach Hause gehen!"* or simply, *"Ich will nach Hause!"*

Our hearts reached out to him. He was rather tall for his age, but his boyish face and voice betrayed his tender years. His clean uniform indicated that he had not seen much combat. Probably he had been conscripted within the previous days or, at most, weeks, put into a uniform, and told to go out and defend his native city.

When he pathetically beseeched us again, "I will to go home!" I could stand it no longer. I went over to him and explained, "You cannot go home, you are a prisoner of war." I hated having to say that. We all wanted to go home.

Then this soldier lad said, "Mein Onkel at Ann Arbor. Mein Onkel at Ann Arbor." Ann Arbor, I recalled, was the home of the University of Michigan. "Does you uncle teach at the University of Michigan?" I asked, and he replied, "Yes."

One of the older men who had surrendered apparently had begun to celebrate the occasion before our arrival. In his inebriated condition everybody, German or American, was hail fellow well met.

One of the older men in our platoon, a man about thirty years of age, was Charlie Kile from Muncie, Indiana. Charlie was an accountant in civilian life and worked for a loan company in Muncie. He was always level headed, patient and cool, even in the rigors of combat, but he soon tired of our German friend's exuberance and told him to sit down by the side of the road and be quiet. There was a communication problem to be sure; the German ignored Charlie and kept making noise. At this point, the man from Indiana lost his patience, fired his rifle into the bank of dirt next to the prisoner and repeated his instructions. With eyes as big as saucers the German looked at Charlie in awe, sat down by the bank of the road and remained quiet. The party was over.

We stood around for about twenty minutes waiting for a detail to come and take the prisoners away. The rest of the company was up ahead a short distance, waiting for orders to move on into Hohenlimburg. Finally, when several G.I.'s showed up to take the prisoners, I almost hated to see them go. Perhaps it was a possessive feeling but they had surrendered to *us,* not to some other outfit behind the lines. As for the fifteen year old boy, I wanted to say, "Be kind to him."

I hope the lad made it home, even though he probably had to spend some time as a prisoner of war. His plaintive request struck a responsive chord in our hearts. War may seem glamourous from a distance but when you're in it, you just "will" to go home.

A soldier's prayer, usually spoken lightly, often was, "Dear Lord, I don't want to be a hero, I just want to go home." The lightness could not conceal the sincerity behind it.

I don't mean to imply that we had no heroes in our company. We certainly did, and plenty of them. Several of our men laid down their lives for their country. Two men received battlefield commissions and two others received the Silver Star, one of them posthumously. There were Bronze Stars too and at least twenty-five Purple Hearts.[2]

We had one man, one of the college boys, John W. Heisy from Pennsylvania,[3] who frankly said he wanted to go home with a Purple Heart. John got his wish. Early one morning, just before daylight, as we advanced openly upon a German gun crew holed up in a large two-story wooden frame house, he was shot in the arm. As he went to the rear, he shouted, "Hey fellas, I got my Purple heart!"

As far as I am concerned now, every man who sticks it out in combat and does his duty is a hero. Nevertheless, the yearning for loved ones and home is always there.

The homing instinct in all creatures is God-given. Even Jesus of Nazareth revealed His longing for a home when

He said to an impulsive new convert, "Foxes have holes, and birds of the air have nests; but the Son of man hath not where to lay his head."[4]

The homing instinct is the texture of human society.[5] It is stronger than the state, it is stronger than war. When the German boy said, "I will to go home!" he was expressing an instinct that begins in a mother's womb. And it grows from the moment of birth.

Many of my war experiences have faded from memory and in some ways, that's good. But the sight and sound of that young, frightened boy remains in my mind forever. No matter what our national origin, there's no place like home.

Chapter 15

Hohenlimburg
The Choir on the Hill

*"The things of the Spirit of God ... They are
spiritually discerned."*
—I Corinthians 2:14.

After the prisoners were taken away we continued to
wait a little while before moving ahead into Hohenlimburg.
There was a bend in the road up ahead and those of us farther back could not see what was transpiring at the head of
the column.

I remember wondering what was going on, yet not feeling
in a hurry—we knew what was eventually in store for us.
Soon the familiar call came down the line: "Let's go."

Richard A. Briggs has written, "The 342nd Infantry ...
continued its advance on April 15, with its First and Second
Battalions pressing on Hohenlimburg, an industrial city near
the Lenne River. The 2nd Bn., 342 Inf. entered Hohenlimburg
at 1300 and after an afternoon of house to house fighting,
secured the city at 1730."[1] Our company, Company "E," was
part of the Second Battalion.

Except for blurred recollections, especially of the sound
of artillery shells crashing, the house to house fighting mentioned
by Briggs seems to have sunk into some kind of "memory

hole." Perhaps I should be thankful for that. However, the grace of God has preserved for me the memory of one incident which remains intact.

It was getting late in the afternoon and the artillery shells seemed to be exploding just beyond the buildings on our left front. On our right was a large rectangular building. We forced our way into its reception area and Captain Hensley shouted to a clerk behind a desk that everyone was to clear the building. The poor fellow became flustered and I wondered if he even understood, but he must have gotten the message. He moved very quickly. At the same time the captain took several of the men with him to go through the building and clear it of any remaining occupants and possible resistance.

The people streamed out, terror etched on the faces of some of them. Our orders were to take them across the street and make them wait in a group on a grassy knoll overlooking the building and the surrounding area. There were about fifty of them altogether, both men and women. Those of us who guarded them remained at the base of the hill or on the road outside the building.

In the midst of the affray I began to feel some concern. The position of the people was precarious; one stray shell could destroy them all, not to mention ourselves. I hoped the captain and the other fellows would not be long.

Then a remarkable thing happened, something totally unexpected. With one person leading them, a woman wearing religious habit, the German civilians on the hill began to sing. It was obvious that they had sung together before, either as a congregation or as a choir.

I could not understand what they were singing—and there was plenty of competition in the background. But these were clearly songs of faith, not songs of war. Perhaps they were German hymns or, when they spoke in unison, passages of Scripture or portions of their liturgy. Whatever it was they were singing, the spiritual tone was plain and clear while the strength of their voices seemed to roll down the hill like a wave.

I listened in amazement and admiration that they could do this—would even dare to do it—and I must acknowledge now, my heart was touched. We were on opposite sides of a great struggle but in that evening air a stronger force was at work. I became one in heart and spirit with the Christians on the hill.

No doubt we had interrupted their Sunday evening vespers. They continued outside, their faith lifting them above the battle strife—the shells bursting nearby and the enemy soldiers guarding them.

All this time my anxiety kept increasing. Finally I heard a shout from the front of the building, "Bring them in!" I looked over and one of the fellows was standing there waving his arms. I turned, waved to the people, and shouted, "Let's go back in!"

As the people streamed back through the lobby I watched their faces intently. I remember one young woman, still wringing her hands, tears coursing down her cheeks, and her face twisted with fright. She appeared to be the only one. Most of the others I could observe were certainly relieved but still calm and resolute. One older man impressed me a great deal. He was of medium height and dressed impeccably in a brown tweed suit. He held himself proudly and erect. I was standing to the left of the people as they marched in. His head turned slightly toward me and our eyes met. They bespoke a casual and placid defiance, as if to say, "Now, if you don't mind, we shall go on with what we were doing."

I wanted in some way to communicate with these people,

to express my own relief and admiration for their courage and faith, but such a thing was out of the question. I could only return their glances. I learned in that moment that there is a great difference between being conquered and being vanquished.

The whole episode is a memory I have cherished all these years and shared with a few friends and loved ones. Now I feel I must record it, lest it remain untold forever.

It is possible, I believe, for an unusual experience to become a "cup of strength" in a time of great agony.[2] Throughout the years that is the way I have felt about that moment in Hohenlimburg. I hope that is also the way some of those German civilians have felt. Standing in the open, in the very midst of shot and shell, they sang songs of faith. Perhaps none of them realized how much they touched the heart of a young American soldier guarding them.

The things of the Spirit know no boundaries. It is in the realm of the flesh that barriers and hostilities exist between nations and peoples. For this we pay a heavy price.

The 342nd Infantry achieved its objective that evening. Hohenlimburg fell to the Americans. By April 17 all German resistance throughout the Ruhr came to an end.[3]

Historians have written about the Allied victory in that part of western Germany. One writer describes the role of the 86th Blackhawk Division as "10 days of fierce and sometimes brutal fighting against Germany's best."[4] Today, after fifty years, I feel a measure of pride at having been a soldier in that campaign. But my feelings go deeper than mere pride. I realize the true value of the experience.

I also learned that afternoon in Hohenlimburg, as in so many of my experiences in the Ruhr, that God is always victorious. Many members of the choir on the hill must have felt that they experienced a spiritual victory. Their faith had given them triumph in a time of great danger.

In my own heart and mind I experienced a force that told me there is a power in the world stronger than the enmity of nations at war—a power that can bind the hearts of men. It is our Christian faith and "the things of the Spirit of God."[5]

Chapter 16

Three Days in Hohenlimburg
(and the Rape of the Drape)

We spent three days and nights in Hohenlimburg, April 15-17, leaving for Bavaria late on the afternoon of April 18th. In my memory now the time there has become a montage of experiences, almost a kaleidoscope. To put them all in proper sequence is virtually impossible. But this does not lessen their vividness or reality in my mind.

We took over some of the German homes and Johnnie Jernigan and I found ourselves on the third floor of a large three-story box-like wooden structure. Our quarters had drapes on the windows and a beautiful double bed. It was a combination living room and bedroom. After being in the cold and mud for ten days, it was pure luxury.

Johnnie cast his eyes on those drapes and suggested that a piece of one would make a beautiful scarf or muffler, something to keep a soldier warm on cold nights in the open air. After two days I could no longer dissuade him. He took his bayonet and knife and carved out a piece of material from one of the drapes. It did make a colorful addition to an otherwise drab combat uniform.

"Our house" stood at the end of a row of houses and next to a road which ran along the foot of a steep forested mountain. On this road at the base of the mountain, and not far from our front door, rested a huge blown-out German Panzer tank. It served as a constant reminder of the battle which had just ended. Each time I walked by it I wondered if someone was still inside, asleep in death.

About a quarter of a mile down this road at the base of the mountain was another cluster of houses and also a large open space on the other side of a stream. It was there that the German troops gathered by the thousands as they came in to surrender.

Directly across the street in front of our house was an open gravely area about the size of several city lots. Across this area flowed the stream which I have mentioned above. It was shallow but rather wide and rocky. I didn't ask the name of it, I think now it must have been the Lenne River on which the city of Hohenlimburg was situated.

During our first full day in Hohenlimburg thousands of German troops came in to the area to surrender. They gathered near the cluster of houses about a half mile away. Some of them came in on foot, others were driving their vehicles. I was impressed with their uniforms; some of them had fur-lined garments and I envied them their warmth. My first impression was that the German people must have donated their household fur garments to the men in uniform.

One of the German soldiers was wearing a beautiful black leather jacket. It was a short and rather sporty thing. One of the young fellows in our squad, whose name I do not remember for sure, took a liking to that jacket, "borrowed" it and wore it around during the day as we moved about among our own men and the Germans. He was also possessed with a dash of bravado and was wearing a pistol on each hip, pistols which he had acquired somewhere along the way during the Ruhr fighting. As he strutted about among the troops, both American and German, one of the German soldiers stood eyeing him with an air of amusement. I was standing nearby watching this bit of action when the German, an older man, noticed me. Pointing at my young buddy, he exclaimed with just one word and a smile, "Chicago!" Apparently this German had seen his share of 1930-vintage gangster movies.

The next day an order came down from the regimental commander, "No American soldier shall wear any portion of a German uniform." That was the end of my young buddy's dashing leather jacket. He handed it over to one of the German soldiers.

During that day, as the Germans kept drifting in and we were guarding some of them who had been moved into a large enclosure across the stream, two young German teenagers walked up to me smiling rather pleasantly though sheepishly. They handed me a sheet of yellow paper which resembled a telegram. It contained a typewritten message addressed to the Americans. It identified the two young boy-soldiers by name and their military organization. It then proceeded to say that they had been honorably discharged from their unit and were now civilians. Please allow them to go home. It was signed by their company commander.

I looked at the boys and then I looked at that piece of paper. That was a moment when I wished I was a four-star general and could tell them to go on home. I explained to the boys that I could not do anything about the message from their company commander; they would have to join the other prisoners. They did not seem too upset about it. I smiled at their effort to return as quickly as possible to civilian life. They smiled too and walked over and took their place with the other German prisoners.

That same night our squad, just twelve of us, had its turn at guarding the several hundred German soldiers who had been placed in the enclosure by the stream. I have often wondered what we could have done if they had all just decided to walk away, twelve of us guarding hundreds, if not thousands, of them. We would have had quite a time rounding them up. But docile and obedient, they remained in the enclosure behind one or two strands of wire, apparently thankful that for them at least the war was over.

As the evening wore on and the air became cool some of the prisoners gathered in groups and began to sing. It was obviously an effort to lift their spirits. I did not recognize what they were singing; perhaps they were German folk songs. I must admit they were all rather pretty. Under different circumstances I might have enjoyed the concert more.

A few of the prisoners came over to the strands of wire which separated us and asked, *"Is der Krieg fertig?* "Is the war finished?"

There was sadness and resignation in their voices. We explained that we had heard the Russians were in Berlin and it looked like the war was just about over. A look of despair came over the faces of several of them. We gave them the cigarettes and food items from our "K" rations, which they accepted with thanks.

During the course of the evening one of the fellows in our platoon came over to where we were with an unusual request for help. He and some of the other men were guarding the German officers who had been placed in a house across the road from the enclosure or compound. Also, they were guarding a small contingent of women who, we were told, had been with the German troops. These women were in the same house with the officers but had been consigned to a separate room. The women, my buddy explained, were asking permission to go to the toilet and he did not know how to tell them, "one at a time."

I wasn't sure of the German idiom for *one at a time* but I went over with him to the house where the women were being kept. Some of them came to the doorway and I tried to explain that only one could go to the toilet at a time. One of the women then smiled pleasantly, held up a finger as though giving me a language lesson, and told me to say, *"Immer ein"* ("always one"). That seemed to make things clear. The ladies then agreed that they would leave the room only one at a time.

After that brief episode I walked with my buddy into their adjoining room where the German officers were being kept. The room was dimly lit by lanterns which added to the scene of total dejection and despair. These officers, still clad in their military uniforms, were sitting around on sofas and in large easy chairs. Their heads were down and they were leaning on their elbows, some of them trying to sleep. Women from the German Red Cross, dressed in white uniforms, were waiting on them, bringing them warm drinks.

I stood there for a moment, looking around the room. One of the Red Cross Women stopped what she was doing and looked back at me. I felt completely out of place. I knew what she was thinking: "Must you come in and add to the tragedy of this spectacle?" I took one more glance around the room and then quietly slipped away.

After that Johnnie Jernigan, our squad leader, came and got me. Johnnie had been sitting in an adjoining house with a German officer. The other officers, Johnnie explained, would have nothing to do with this man. They did not even want him in the same room with them and so he was placed in the house nearby and Johnnie had been put there with him to guard him—if it could be called guarding.

"He wants to talk, Sid," Johnnie said, "but I can't tell what he's got on his mind." I listened to this odd-man-out for a while and responded as best I could, but finally had to admit I could not be sure what was bothering him. Johnnie and I could only conclude that he had done something that made the other German officers despise and ostracize him. It was their problem and we could not help.

About eleven or twelve o'clock (2300 or 2400 army time) we were allowed to go back to the house and sleep for several hours while some other members of our company relieved us. However, we were back early in the morning to again guard the men in the large enclosure. They had made it through the night and many of them were down at the edge of the stream washing their faces in the cool water. Yes, "war is hell" and "there are no winners in warfare." These are the cliches we often hear. But as we look upon all the tragedy associated with defeat, we cannot help but realize there are advantages to being on the winning side.

One scene from those three or four days in Hohenlimburg remains vividly in my mind. The German troops had stacked their rations or food supplies in one particular spot in that open area where we were on duty guarding prisoners. This included a huge stack of canned supplies. I noticed an America officer, a major, and a German officer walking around together obviously concerned with the food and the feeding of the multitude of German troops. This made an impression on me, that former enemies could cooperate this way to feed the thousands of men on their hands and prevent further tragedy. Perhaps we can say it was a little token of things to come in the postwar years.

At the same time those cans of German rations looked rather appealing to a couple of us. I suggested we walk over, open one of the cans, and have a sample. However, the meat was cold and greasy and we could not eat it. We replaced the lid and put the can back in the stack.

Some of the fellows in our company had an unusual experience which I can only relate as it was told to me. It occurred either the night we arrived in Hohenlimburg or early the next morning. As I recall, it included our platoon sergeant, Dominic DePhillips from Chicago.

Our men heard shouts coming from a wooded area. Sensing that it was Germans and not knowing what their intentions were, they sent rifle fire in that direction. This only brought forth more shouts, obviously angry now, and getting closer. Finally they could see and understand a German soldier who was leading his comrades out of the woods. "What's the matter with you guys?" he asked, "can't you understand English? Don't you know what the word *'surrender'* means?"

This man's English had a familiar ring. It was Brooklynese and to the astonishment of our men, he was from Brooklyn, New York. Needless to say, his surrender and that of his buddies was accepted without further complications or perhaps I should say misunderstandings.

By the third afternoon the German soldiers had all been taken away and things seemed rather quiet in Hohenlimburg. Now, for the first time in weeks, I reflected on how dirty I was. There wasn't much I could do about my uniform but I thought about my socks and underwear. They were indescribable and my mind turned to the stream of flowing water across the gravely field. Although it was very cold, at least I had some of the yellow G.I. soap and that might help matters. So I went to the stream with my laundry in hand, a small package of dirty G.I. underwear and socks.

My method of washing was to wet the clothing, rub the soap into them, and then pound them on the rock as I had heard people in other lands did. It seemed to work.

While there a little German girl of about eight or nine suddenly appeared at my side and watched me. (Perhaps she had some suggestions to make, I'm not sure.) I was surprised her mother would let her wander down there alone and observe an enemy soldier, a member of a foreign invasion army, but we fell into a sort of conversation. "Can you speak any English?" I asked her in German, and she replied, "*Ich kann gar nichts Englisch sprechen.*" (I can't speak any English.) To this day I remember that phrase. Like another one, "*Ist der Krieg fertig?*" (Is the war over?) It has remained in my mind all these years.

There was one more thing of the utmost importance we could do when things quieted down in Hohenlimburg, and that was write letters home. To me that meant a letter home to Jo. We had been married only a few weeks when the orders came that took us overseas to combat. While crossing the Atlantic there was time and opportunity to write. Also there was time in France. Since entering combat there was little or no opportunity. Also, when we did find time to write we were under orders not to give any information about our whereabouts or what we were doing—in short, we could not even say that we had been in combat. That privilege would come later when we were in Bavaria. I felt very inhibited as I attempted to write and I'm sure the other men felt the same way. There was so much we would have liked to have said but orders were orders. One thing we learn from an experience like that: the privilege, even the joy of freedom of expression.

On the afternoon of April 18th we loaded everything into our field packs and prepared to leave Hohenlimburg. Our entire company sat along both sides of the street in front of our house and strung out around the nearby corner. It was a warm and pleasant afternoon but I remember the eerie quiet which seemed to have settled over everything. The German soldiers had all been taken away and at the moment no civilians were to be seen anywhere.

We had been waiting for a long time for the trucks, so it seemed, when suddenly from out of nowhere two young German men appeared. They were certainly in their late twenties or early thirties, were dressed in dark suits and white shirts and ties, and each one wore a boutonniere, a white flower, in his coat lapel. We gazed at them in astonishment. They were a sight we hadn't seen since civilian life before the war. It was as though they appeared from another world, a world we had forgotten existed.

They walked down the middle of the road between our rows of men, with only an occasional glance sideways at us. At first not a soul in our company said a word—we could only stare. Then suddenly Sergeant John R. Gellatly from Bridgeport, Connecticut, blurted out, "Hey, where are you guys going? To a wedding?" They glanced toward Gellatly but did not respond. I felt they did not understand. No one else said a word and no one challenged them or heckled them although it seemed to me they were walking a gauntlet of foreign soldiers. Soon they were out of sight. I think we all wondered, "How could this strange sight be?"

For fifty years I have wondered where the two German men were going, dressed so formally in their dark suits. Sergeant Gellatly only shouted what we were all thinking. As I reflect now on that experience I believe they were going to a funeral, not a wedding, for there had been much death in Hohenlimburg during the preceding week.

The two German men were hardly out of sight when a tall slender German woman appeared, a woman in her fifties or early sixties. This too was a surprise. She came from around the corner where the two men had gone and she was obviously concerned, determined, and in a hurry. We watched her intently and to my surprise, almost horror, she entered the house where Johnnie and I had been staying. My heart sank; I thought of those beautiful drapes.

In a few moments the woman came charging out of the house. Distress and anger were written all over her face. Johnnie was sitting on the curb not far from me, the beautiful muffler around his neck. I held my breath and tried to blend into the landscape. But the German woman raced on past us, going in the direction whence she had come. I heaved a sigh of relief. We had faced German artillery and rifle fire, but I did not want to face the wrath of that German woman.

I learned a lesson about bravery from that experience. We had faced German artillery and rifle fire, even advanced openly against it, but I did not want to face the wrath of the German woman. What was the difference?

Bravery must have some sort of foundation, a conviction of right or justice. We risked our lives, not only because we were trained to do so but because we believed our cause was just. In destroying the drape there was no such conviction.

Part III

Across Bavaria with General Patton

Chapter 17

My Ambulance to Bavaria

Dusk was settling over Hohenlimburg when the trucks finally appeared. The war was over for some people but not for us.

As the men climbed aboard, Captain Hensley noticed that one of the fellows in our platoon was drunk and wobbling around in a silly way. He proceeded to give him a tongue lashing, not because it was a moral issue but because a drunk soldier is a menace and a problem.

It is hard to be judgmental in such situations. This buddy of ours was evidence that Solomon was right when he wrote, "Wine is a mocker, strong drink is raging."[1] Yet, as I listened to the captain bawl him out and watched the look on the soldier's face, I couldn't help but feel sorry for him. He wasn't so drunk but what he knew he was on the receiving end of verbal fireworks—and Captain Hensley could dish out the fireworks when the situation called for it.

What makes a decent and friendly young man do what this soldier did? Perhaps the stress and strain of combat finally got to him. Now there was, for him at least, the terrifying prospect of more.

As the men loaded onto the trucks, I realized that I was sick. My problem was diarrhea, the bane of the infantryman, and we never knew when it would strike.

The prospect of bouncing along in an army truck all night and on into the next day was more than I could tolerate. Nearby I noticed a captured German army truck, a Ford V-8, which was now a part of our convoy and was being driven by two of our men. The back was loaded with our field packs and other equipment. This was my opportunity. With a "go ahead" from the drivers, I climbed aboard and made a makeshift bed for myself among the packs. That German truck became my ambulance all the way to Bavaria.

It was 230 miles from Hohenlimburg to the area of Würzburg where we were to join General Patton's Third Army the next day. It rained much of the night and the back of the truck was not covered, but I managed somehow to tolerate it down among the packs. Also, according to Briggs, when we were near Frankfurt a lone German plane strafed the entire column and wrecked the nerves of everyone.[2] I never noticed. Perhaps I slept through this incident; on the other hand I was probably too sick to care. Every time the convoy stopped, I climbed down from the truck and there beside the road, without any embarrassment, relieved my diarrhea.

During the afternoon of April 19 the 86th Division arrived in the assembly area near Würzburg. That evening we became members of the Third Army.

We were in an area of Germany known as Franconia.[3] Here is located the medieval city Rothenburg on the Tauber, still protected by its massive walls and today one of Germany's most popular tourist attractions.

The rolling countryside was beautiful—farms, forests, small villages, and people working in the fields. During our several days in this area there was little contact with German units.[4] This provided opportunity for less combative activities—resting, writing letters home, and even some foraging to seek a change of fare. During this time we learned to say *"Haben Sie Eier?"* "Have you any eggs?" and our diet was augmented with fresh German farm produce.

In the meantime General Patton had learned that he would not be permitted to advance his forces beyond the Elbe River in central Europe, thus frustrating his drive toward Berlin. As a result he decided on a two-pronged attack eastward, one into Czechoslovakia and the other southeastward through the heart of Bavaria. The purpose of this thrust was to liquidate any German last stand in the mountains of southern Germany and Austria.[5]

It was to this drive through Bavaria that the 86th Division was committed. We were to go on a general offensive and our immediate goal was to cross the Danube River and there establish a bridgehead.[6]

Chapter 18

The Attack on Ingolstadt
(with Music in the Afternoon)

"He maketh me to lie down in green pastures."
—Psalm 23:2

A group of us stood on high ground gazing at Ingolstadt in the distance. Between us and the city lay several miles of lush green fields. We had to cross those fields in order to capture Ingolstadt.

We had advanced to the southern fringe of the Franconian uplands. Ingolstadt was situated below us in a wide plain of the Danube Valley.[1]

A young German boy, about twelve years of age, stood with us, telling us about the splendors and wonders of the city in the distance. I marveled, and still do, that he showed no animosity toward us.

The sight of Ingolstadt was indeed something to talk about. It was a pleasant spring morning with a touch of haze in the air. This seemed to add a touch of drama to the moment. The destruction which the city had experienced by warfare was blurred by the haze and the distance between us, and the buildings, spires and towers stood out as silhouettes.

In an hour the order came to "move out" and we started across the open countryside. The Danube River flowed through one part of Ingolstadt and that was our objective.

We were tired and I remember actually praying for a moment of sleep. But there was no time for that. We were a small part of General Patton's drive across Bavaria and there was no tarrying along the way.

As we approached the city I saw in the distance some German soldiers jumping into a truck and hurrying away. Perhaps they had set a booby trap for us as a part of our reception. Then we were greeted by shellfire and the order came to scatter out and lie down in the grass.

We lay in that field for over an hour. We could not see the man nearest to us, so occasionally we shouted at one another to be sure the others had not moved away and left us there.

The grass was about a foot high—the tender new grass of spring—and the afternoon was warm. A drowsiness crept over me and there were moments when I dozed off, only to be awakened by a timely German shell. Those moments proved to be what I needed, as a long evening and night lay ahead.

As I lay in that field the words of the twenty-third Psalm came to mind—"He maketh me to lie down in green pastures"—and I began to realize the anomaly of the situation. I had muttered a prayer for sleep but never expected my prayer to be answered in this way.

There were moments during the quiet interludes when I was certain I heard music in the distance. It seemed to come in waves, perhaps influenced by the afternoon breeze. But such a thing was incredible. I doubted my ears and I doubted the experience.

I said nothing to anyone about hearing music that afternoon. And strangely enough, none of the other men mentioned it to me. It became for me a secret which I kept for forty years until I learned about Richard A. Brigg's book.

In *Black Hawks Over the Danube* Briggs tells about that afternoon on the outskirts of Ingolstadt. Himself a rifleman in the 86th Division, he describes how we were halted by heavy mortar and artillery fire. As we tried to move forward, German sound trucks could be heard in the distance. They were playing Strauss waltzes in an effort to stir patriotism in the defenders of the Danube River line.[2]

Later that afternoon we were able to enter the city and Ingolstadt fell to the Americans. We paused for a while, even rested in German homes, before setting out for the river's edge.

This evening pause gave me an opportunity to brush my teeth, something sorely needed, for I had lost my toothbrush two or three days before, and this was having an effect upon my morale. At the risk of disgusting some readers I will relate how this was accomplished. In a German home I spotted a neat row of toothbrushes. After consideration of the risk involved, I took one of them, washed it in order to sanitize it, and brushed my teeth, using the rough bar of soap at hand for tooth paste. I then washed it again and placed it back in the rack.

I thought of "liberating" that toothbrush, but one of my buddies reminded me that no doubt that was all the family had. They could not get another. For the moment at least my mouth felt clean and my morale was definitely improved. When the battle to cross the Danube was over I was able to acquire a new toothbrush.

It was midnight and very dark when we crossed the Danube River on a pontoon foot bridge which somehow the engineers had managed to put down. The Germans were shelling us heavily and as we went across it seemed that shells were exploding all around us. But the orders were to put your head down and run as fast as you can.

The units which preceded us had a more difficult time. Company "K" led the attack for our regiment, the 342nd. When they reached the middle of the stream German mortar fire made direct hits on several of the boats.[3] This resulted in heavy casualties, one of whom was my friend, Eugene Roddy, who had served as best man in our wedding the previous December in San Luis Obispo. During the months that followed Gene recovered from his wounds.

When Company "E" got across the Danube we climbed up the opposite bank of the river and rushed into a massive fort which had been built by King Ludwig I of Bavaria in the 1800s.[4] Fortunately for us, the fort had been taken by "F" and "G" companies attacking side by side.[5]

The battle to cross the Danube continued during much of the night and, at various points along the river, on into the daylight hours. But during the morning the beachhead across the river was made secure.

In 1982, in the company of our oldest son, Dr. David Hatch, my wife and I returned to Ingolstadt. We located the old fort and stood on the east bank of the Danube River at the very point where our company came across the night of April 26-27, 1945. The intervening years had not erased the memories of that moment.

Near us were the massive walls of the large fort which our regiment, the 342nd Infantry, captured during that engagement. My wife took pictures which we shared with others upon our arrival home.

One evening as we showed our slides of Ingolstadt to family members, our five-year-old grandson, Alex Chapman, gazed at the pockmarked walls of the German fort and asked, "Grandpa, were any men killed?" "Yes, Alex," I replied,

The massive fort

Where the Danube was crossed from the east side in 1945

Pockmarked walls of the German fort

"There were many casualties."

Alex thought for a moment and then asked, "Are you one of the survivors?" "Yes," I said, "I am one of the survivors."

Again Alex became very thoughtful. Then he looked at me and said quite seriously, "I'm glad, because if you hadn't been one of the survivors, I wouldn't have had a grandpa."

The experiences at Ingolstadt remain among the most impressive of my combat days with "the Blackhawks." They are a cluster of memories—the German boy who wanted to tell us all about the city, the afternoon when German artillery made us lie down in the grassy fields and rest awhile, the toothbrush incident, of which I am not boasting, and the race across the pontoon bridge at midnight.

They all mean something to me now. However, I especially cherish the afternoon in the grassy field when I got the sleep I prayed for. God's Word is true, "He maketh me to lie down in green pastures."

Chapter 19

Death in a Garden of Roses
(A Parable of Mankind)

*"The LORD God planted a garden . . .
and there he put the man."*
—Genesis 2:8.

As we moved up to the banks of the Danube, preparatory to crossing and seizing the huge fort on the other side, one of our officers, Lieutenant William G. Gill from San Antonio, Texas, remarked aloud, "I understand that 'G' Company has secured the fort."

Lieutenant Gill spoke with an air of relief. "That's good," I responded. I, too, spoke with relief.

The other companies, along with the artillery, had indeed softened up the fort, although not without casualties. When Company "E" got across the river we clambered up the bank and rushed through its gates, meeting little or no resistance. Thinking the fort was now ours, and all was secure, we even tried to rest for a while in bunks previously occupied by German troops.

With the advent of daylight, however, firing broke out again in another sector of the vast complex. In the excitement and confusion that ensued, I found myself running through a beautiful rose garden.

Suddenly I stopped. I had almost stumbled over a man lying on the ground. He was resplendent in his uniform, his black German army boots were polished to perfection, and he was obviously a handsome man. However, one side of his head was blown completely open and his brains were spilled out upon the ground. I looked at him and exclaimed aloud, "Poor fellow!"—an exclamation which as a child I had heard my mother use when confronted by the sight of a human tragedy.

The contradictions of the circumstances got to me: the garden, the roses in full bloom, and a human being lying dead with his brains blown out. Then in that moment I realized I had better keep moving. A moving target is more difficult to hit.

In my mind I have formulated two possible scenarios for the German officer lying there. Perhaps, in an hour of despair, with the fort falling to the Americans, he had gone alone to the rose garden to take his life, rather than surrender. However, I cannot now recall that there was a pistol on the ground near him. Another possibility is that he was taken there and executed by his own men. Such things do happen in warfare.

When the firing which began at daylight finally ceased, we witnessed an incredible sight. Across the open area from us, a German company of about a hundred men marched out in formation. They were followed by two American G.I.s brandishing pistols. When the fighting in the fort finally ended a total of 430 German soldiers had surrendered[1]

But it was the sight of the German officer upon the ground that made a searing impression upon my mind. There it would remain for the rest of my life.

It was in a beautiful garden that death first laid hold of humankind. There in Eden, Adam and Eve disobeyed God and from that garden they were expelled, that they might not have access to the Tree of Life and Live forever.[2]

In another garden a decision was made that would change forever the history of the world. It was in Gethsamane that Jesus of Nazareth surrendered to the will of God.[3] Now in the place where He was crucified there was a garden, and in the garden a new sepulcher in which no one had ever been laid. There He was buried and there He rose from the dead.[4]

Finally, in a garden of tomorrow there will be no more death. The former things will have passed away.[5]

For many years I reflected on that moment in the garden of roses in the old fort in Ingolstadt. We don't immediately understand God's message in many things that occur in our lives. In time, however, the sight of the German officer in the garden came to be for me a parable of the death versus life history of the human race. The greatest crises in this age-long struggle are associated with gardens.

Chapter 20

The Soldier's Prize
(and the Hungarians)

"I rejoice at thy word, as one that findeth great spoil."
—Psalm 119:162

When the fighting ended in the old fort in Ingolstadt, a few of us, curious as to what we might find, wandered farther on into its innermost recesses.

We walked across an open area inside the fort's walls and stood in a garage where the German troops obviously serviced and repaired their motor vehicles. From there I noticed some faces peeking out of the entranceway to a series of bunkers. These bunkers were actually structures reinforced by earth pushed up against them so that they gave the appearance of being semi-underground.

Lieutenant Keeton, our platoon leader, was with us. I offered to go to the bunkers and call to the people inside to come out, if he and the others would cover me with their rifles. I raced across the remaining open area, stood just to the side of the entrance and began to call to those inside. They were not long in responding.

The people streamed out, men, women and bicycles, perhaps seventy-five of them altogether. With smiles on their faces they kept exclaiming *"Ungar! Ungar! Ungar!"* These were Hungarians. The men were in brown uniforms which, I assume, was the uniform of Hungarian troops which had fought alongside the Germans. Several of them had ostrich feathers in their hats. It was such a pleasant surprise to what could have happened that I smiled back at them and acknowledged their identity with exclamations of *"Ungar!"* Some of our men then came forward and escorted them away.

At this point another soldier and I decided to go in and explore the long line of bunkers out of which the Hungarians had come. We moved cautiously from one room to another, passing bins of potatoes, food supplies and other materials. Suddenly we stopped and stared in amazement. We had come upon a huge store of German Luger pistols, something coveted by almost every combat soldier. And there was plenty of ammunition to go with them.

Now we faced the problem which confronts every foot soldier; we could not carry our huge cache with us. We could only strap on one Luger in a shoulder holster, take some ammunition and hurry back out of the bunkers lest the company go on without us.

In the "Book of Psalms" there is a verse which says, "I rejoice at thy word, as one that findeth great spoil."[1] Here the Psalmist draws upon the battlefield experience of a soldier. There is the agony of the conflict and the danger of the battle, but it ends with the reward of the spoil."[2]

During my years in the Christian ministry I have on more than one occasion found something in the Scriptures that has kindled my interest or even excited me. It is the joy of discovery all over again and my mind goes back to that experience as a soldier a long time ago. I understand the emotion of the Psalmist when he wrote, "I rejoice at thy word, as one that findeth great spoil."

My buddy and I hurried back to the company, shared

with them the excitement of our discovery and displayed our prizes. But my Luger and I were soon to part company. One night in combat my rifle had failed to function semiautomatically so I bartered my Luger for another pistol (of lesser repute) and along with it a cleaning rod. When combat ended I sold this second pistol to one of the other men.

With the end of the war in Europe our division was granted thirty-day furloughs at home in the States before being sent to the Philippines. I still had in my pocket the money from the sale of the second pistol. With that money my wife and I rented an apartment for a week at Huntington Beach, California. It was the honeymoon we had not had before I went overseas.

Do I regret not keeping my Luger pistol and bringing it home? Such questions occur to us in these days of violence on the home front. No, it has been more meaningful to me to have the memory of the experience, the added insight and joy certain passages of Scripture bring, and a wonderful honeymoon.

Chapter 21

An Encounter with the Geneva Convention
(My Hardest Job in Combat)

"Thou shalt not covet thy neighbor's house."
—Exodus 20:17
"For a man's house is his castle."
—Sir Edward Coke (1552-1634)

"If you are going to major in history, you should take French or German."

These were the words of my counsellor as I met with him to plan my first year in college. It was the fall of 1936 and the place was Pasadena, California. There at what is now Pasadena City College I began my college career.

I really didn't care which language I took and almost blurted out "French." But then I felt restrained for a moment and thought, "Why not German?"

My mother had often said *Gute Nacht* and *Guten Morgen* to us children. And she had taught us such expressions as *Auf Wiedersehen, Ich liebe dich* and, of course, *Ja* and *Nein*. These were a part of her heritage and she passed it on to us.

All this passed through my mind in a moment of time and I said to the counsellor, "It'll be German." Little did I realize the role this decision would play in my life a few years hence.

The freshman course in German was difficult and I struggled at first. Again my mother's background helped—this time not to make a decision but just to survive. Seeing my struggle, she took me in tow and showed me that I had to get in and learn those vocabularies, declensions, and conjugations. She had never studied German in the classroom but a major in Latin at a woman's college[2] in the South gave her the know-how.

We learned things the old fashioned way in those days. A firm and strict teacher permitted no casual sloughing off. It made the difference.

Nine years later I stood in the living room of a German home, rifle slung over my shoulder, and said to the father, "You must vacate your house. American soldiers are going to sleep here tonight."

We slept in different places each night—out in the open, in a barn, or perhaps not at all, for much of the time we were on the move. Sometimes we evicted the German people from their homes, or from the best rooms of their houses, and slept there ourselves.

On more than one occasion this latter assignment fell to my lot. The order would come from the captain, but it was a policy which, I am sure, must have originated from higher up.

Evicting people was a task I did not enjoy—even hated, "Where shall we go?" they would exclaim, and I would try to ease the pain by suggesting a public building, a local hall, or even the barn—any place I could think of.

This night in particular was especially hard. The weather outside was harsh and the father in the home was not intimidated by my presence. It was a rural area and there were not many places to suggest. When I said, "You must leave," he responded quite firmly, *"Und die Grossmutter?"* ("And the grandmother?")

Seated in a rocking chair in that small living room was an elderly woman. The move obviously would be painful for her, whatever they did, and the challenge in the father's question was clear. On the other hand, I had no authority to make exceptions. I did not dare.

I thought for a moment. A short distance away was the village church. I had noticed it in the afternoon when we arrived there. "The church," I said, "can't all of you go to the church?"

I had not fallen back on this recourse before, but just the mention of the church seemed to lessen the tension and soften the atmosphere. The father thought for a moment, then said, "All right, the church." I turned and walked out. My most difficult encounter, however, was yet to come.

One afternoon several weeks later we entered a Bavarian village. There we stopped. Several of us were standing in the back yard of an impressive three-story brick building, talking and wondering aloud where we would sleep that night. Rumor had it that we were going to occupy that building. This possibility, however, had already become a topic of conversation for we had learned that it was the residence of Roman Catholic nuns.

While we were talking, a messenger brought word from the captain, "It's settled. We are going to stay here. Tell the occupants to leave the building."

I cringed. It was a moment that I had hoped would not materialize. My buddies who were standing with me sensed my discomfort but I had my orders.

I started toward the back of the building, not knowing to whom I would speak. Just then a priest walked around the corner of the building and confronted us. He must have received advance warning of what was about to happen.

"Sir," I said, "the American soldiers are going to sleep here for the night. You must ask the occupants of this building to leave." I employed the best German I could muster.

He looked at me firmly. With a strong voice and perfect English, he replied, "According to the Geneva Convention the occupants of this building do not have to leave. This is their dwelling and that is their right."

I was taken aback. The righteousness of our cause seemed to vanish into thin air. My buddies were watching me; I could see them out of the corner of my eye. I did then what soldiers often do in such circumstances.

"I don't know anything about the Geneva Convention," I said, "but I have my orders." The priest stared at me. Then, with a look of complete disgust, he turned and walked away; he had no choice.

The building was vacated and our infantry company settled in for the night. A fire was built downstairs which warmed the entire structure through its heating system. I was on the third floor and the porcelain pipes which came up into our room became extremely hot. I was able to bake two small potatoes by placing them on one of the pipes. With a dash of salt from our "K" rations, they made a welcomed change of fare. These potatoes had been liberated from a large bin located in one of several wooden sheds behind the convent.

Not everybody felt good about that night and the circumstances of our being there. It is to the credit of some of the Catholic men that they openly expressed their discomfort. Fortunately, we moved on the next day.

Billeting soldiers in civilian homes is a practice that goes back for many centuries.[3] However, the Geneva Conventions do provide for the protection of civilian populations in wartime.[4] And the Ten Commandments say, "Thou shalt not covet thy neighbor's house." Perhaps that is why more than one soldier experienced a certain discomfort that night. The principle is divine and transcends the exigencies of warfare.

We learned many things in our training before going overseas, but evicting civilians from their homes never entered my mind. It was the hardest assignment I had in combat.

Preparation for that responsibility began several years before the war; perhaps in the foreknowledge and providence of God.

Chapter 22

The Password Incarnate
(Lost in a Snow Storm)

"Jesus saith unto him, I am the way,
the truth, and the life."
— John 14:6

In the last week or two of the war we advanced rapidly through Bavaria. Occasionally we encountered resistance, sometimes stiff, but sooner or later we were able to overcome it.

In a rapid advance it is possible for a platoon to get separated from its company or a squad from its platoon. After a time contact is made and men regather. But for some of us in our platoon, one occasion took on ominous tones.

We were riding on tanks that day and realized we had gotten ahead or separated from the other members of our company. We did not take it too seriously, being exhilarated over the collapse of German resistance and thinking in terms of a speedy end to the war. That day, however, the weather became a factor in our advance.

It had been raining during the morning and in the afternoon the rain turned to snow. Within an hour's time the countryside was blanketed in white. During the night the storm would become a raging blizzard sweeping through the Danube Valley.[1]

Our lightheartedness turned into anxiety and concern. We were not only separated, but realized we had lost contact with other American Units.

At dusk we came to a small Bavarian village. We found a large building, a *Gasthaus,* or hotel, and there we took shelter. A group of us stood in the darkened hallway and our platoon leader, Lieutenant William P. Keeton, Jr., from South Hill, Virginia, told us we had better stay put. Other units would surely catch up or find us and then we could decide what to do. In the meantime, sentries must be posted.

Lt. William P. Keeton, Jr

We were confronted by still another problem. To make our isolation more serious, we had not received the password and countersign for the night. To an infantryman in combat, that can mean life or death. And, since I did not know the password and countersign, I could not give it to the soldier whom I would post as a sentry.

The password and countersign were always two unrelated words. For example, if the password was *Omaha,* the countersign could be *tiger,* but it should never be *Nebraska.* The man who was challenged was required to give the password. The sentry then had to respond with the countersign. Failure on the part of either one put him under suspicion as an infiltrator or spy. A new password and countersign were issued each night.

I went out to the edge of the village with another G.I. As I walked back in the darkness a strange voice challenged me and the figure of a soldier whom I did not recognize loomed up before me. Unbeknownst to us, other Americans from a different unit had entered the village.

This newcomer demanded the password which I was unable to give. Not knowing what else to do, I gave the password for the previous night. At this he exclaimed in a trembling voice, "Oh no, no!" and raised his rifle to fire at me. He had every right to do this. For all he knew, I could have been a German infiltrator in American uniform.

"Don't fire!" I cried, and as quickly as I could I explained. We had become separated from our company in the storm, lost all contact with them, and did not get the password. This frightened young comrade believed me, slowly lowered his rifle, and let me through to my platoon.

I have remembered that moment all my life. There can be in human experience such a thing as a word of life. For a moment of time my life depended on a word, the right word, and I did not know it. Is it too much to think that divine intervention spared me the fate which legally could have been dealt out to me?

In the morning we met other members of our company outside the village. Happily, we encountered no more snow storms in our drive across Bavaria.

To me now Christ is the password incarnate,[2] even the door to the kingdom of God. It is through Him and His words that in a future morning we shall join the company of the redeemed and enter into the safety and security of the life to come.

Chapter 23

"Have You Soap?"
(Haircuts in Bavaria)

*"If a [soldier] have long hair, it is
a shame unto him."*
—I Corinthians 11:14.

"Have you soap?" the German boy asked in English. I did not understand him at first, so he repeated himself several times. His pronunciation of the word *soap* was something like *zop*. If he had said "*Seife*," the German word for soap, I would have known what he wanted. Finally I understood.

"Oh, it's soap you want," I exclaimed. "Yes," I assured him, "we have soap."

He explained that they had no soap at home. He would be willing to cut our hair if we would pay him in soap.

I hesitated to accept his proposition. He appeared to be about fourteen or fifteen years of age. I gave him some soap and he went home.

We had stopped in a Bavarian farm village and were relaxing in the afternoon sunshine. There in the courtyard of a "U" shaped complex of farm buildings and a residence the German boy had found us.

He had not been gone more than twenty minutes when he returned and this time his mother was with him. "*Helmut ist ein Friseur"* ("Helmut is a barber", she said. "He has gone to barber school in *München* (Munich). He will be glad to cut your hair if you will pay him in soap.)"

So Helmut was qualified—and he would work for soap. Well, we needed haircuts—and this young mother had a pretty and persuasive smile. How could we pass up a bargain like that?

For the rest of the afternoon Helmut cut hair. He had a set of tools and, it turned out, a professional touch. I don't know how many heads he trimmed, but each time he received payment in soap. Some of the men gave him a whole bar, others a half bar. One or two gave him a piece of the yellowish brown G.I. laundry soap. Whatever it was, he accepted it graciously and with thanks.

In the meantime, in a corner of the complex, another scenario was taking place. At times the voices became rather loud.

In the latter part of the afternoon, while Helmut was still cutting hair, a workman came in with a team of horses and put them in the barn. I assumed he was a member of the German family, perhaps the man of the house, but my guess turned out to be quite wrong.

Some of our fellows, interested in farm animals, went over and watched this man and engaged him in conversation. When they came back in about thirty minutes, they gave the following report.

The man was from one of the east European countries and was working for the German family. (Conversation with him was not difficult for some of our men had east European backgrounds.) This workman liked the German family for which he worked and he did not want to go back to eastern Europe. But he feared that with an American and Allied victory he would be forced to return to his native land. This would mean that he would have to live under communism, something he feared and did not want to do.

The bottom line of the workman's feelings was that he did not look upon us as liberators. And the conversation with our men did not convince him otherwise. It was a sobering new thought to me—I thought everybody welcomed us—and the man's foresight turned out to be true. With the end of hostilities millions in eastern Europe were forced under the yoke of communism.

But now back to Helmut and the more pleasant business of cutting hair. When the young barber finished work that afternoon I'm sure he had enough soap for his own household. Perhaps he and his mother shared it with others in the village.

Life in combat was an earthy business and cleanliness was sometimes a problem. We could shave with a little warm water in a helmet, but had not acquired the trick of cutting our own hair, unless we were willing to let one of our buddies victimize us. Despite our circumstances we did try to keep reasonably clean.

When we got to Austria at the end of the war our entire company was marched to the *Obertrumersee* nearby. There we went swimming, clad quite decently in the fanciest assortment of swim wear imaginable. My own swimming trunks consisted of "long johns" with the legs cut off.

Our squad leader, Johnnie Jernigan, did not wait for the swim in the *Obertrumersee*. A large wash tub was sitting in the yard of the Austrian home where we were billeted. Johnnie filled that tub with water, built a small fire underneath to take the chill off, stripped off his uniform and squeezed in. It was cramped quarters, but he got the job done. When he finished, I changed the water and soaked my wool trousers. At Pfunz in Bavaria I had dived for cover

"F" Company on its way to Obertrum

Orbertrummersee, Austria

in a ditch. Apparently it had also been used as a latrine or dumping hole for human waste. I did not escape unscathed and my trousers still reeked with foul odors.

We were in the army for the duration of the war and six months. Barber shops, baths and showers, clean sheets on a bed and clean clothing in a drawer, seemed far off in time and space.

A haircut in that small Bavarian farm village was a pleasant experience. We learned that afternoon the value of a commodity available to us in our supplies but which we had taken for granted. To this day I think of a bar of soap as a wonderful invention, a real part of modern civilization.

Chapter 24

On the Banks of the Salzach River

(I Can't Get My Breath)

"O the depth of the riches both of the wisdom and knowledge of God! how unsearchable are his judgments, and his ways past finding out!"
—Romans 11:33.

"Pop, go back and ride in one of the jeeps or the truck."

"No," Pop replied, "I'm going to stay with you guys."

Pop, as we called him, was Nelson R. Davis from Hillsboro, New Hampshire. At thirty-nine years of age he was the oldest man in our company and that day he was having difficulty keeping up with the rest of the men.[1] But he was determined and so rejected the suggestion that he ride in one of the vehicles. The suggestion could have been made an order, but if Pop wanted to stay with the other men ... well, so be it, they admired his courage.

It was the last Sunday afternoon of the war. The rumor had gone up and down the line that in the United States people were celebrating the end of hostilities in Europe. We did not know if this rumor was true or how close the end was, but things had been going remarkably well for us—so well, in fact, that we had cast aside our gas masks and entrenching tools.

We were advancing on a narrow road through a forest when we came to the banks of a river. There our rapid advance ground to a halt. If there had been a bridge over the river, it was gone now.

Somebody said we were near the German city of Tittmoning and approaching the border of Austria. Today I know, from studying the maps, that we had reached the banks of the Salzach River, the boundary between Germany and Austria.

The problem was to get across. At the same time we welcomed the opportunity to rest. I relished the thought of just a little time to sit down and get off my feet.

The thought had hardly entered my mind when Captain Hensley ordered Johnnie Jernigan to take his squad and go up the river and dig in. This was a protective measure in case the Germans came across up the river to attack us on the flank. No doubt men were ordered to do the same in the other direction.

Dig in meant digging fox holes at a time when we were dog tired. How lucky, I thought, were the men who got to stay on the road and rest. Why should we be singled out for this? Keeping our grumbling to ourselves, we moved out.

Johnnie took us up the river and placed us strategically along its bank. When he came back to where he had placed me, the first position away from the road, he said he was sure he had seen Germans lurking in the woods across the river. I didn't take him too seriously. It was dusk and I attributed his observations to the flickering shadows of twilight—or his imagination.

Hardly had we positioned ourselves comfortably on the ground when we heard the familiar and terrible whine of German artillery coming our way. We had heard it in Cologne on the Rhine, in the Ruhr fighting and most recently across Bavaria. Now we heard it again. It was something we feared and respected. One more time its shells had zeroed in on us.

At the first sound of the incoming shells Johnnie and I threw ourselves flat on the ground. Then we began to feverishly scrape the earth with our helmets. I took out my pocket knife, opened the large blade, and used it to loosen the top soil. Then we scraped it out with the helmets. Working together, in a few minutes we got several inches below the surface of the ground.

We squeezed into that shallow dugout with the sound of each incoming shell. "Pray, Sid, pray!" Johnnie exclaimed, and I replied, "I'm already praying!"

Then we heard terrible screams from the direction of the road. Johnnie and I looked at each other and knew what had happened. Almost together we said," They've hit the guys on the road."

The exploding shells were tree bursts and extremely dangerous.

The carnage up on the road was awful and the medics were slow in coming up to carry off the casualties. Captain Hensley, enraged, grabbed John F. Wood,[2] his radio man, and the two of them began hauling the wounded men back and away from the area where the shells, with uncanny accuracy, were landing. One man, a young soldier by the name of William P. Kelly, from Shreveport, Louisiana, was observed wandering about in a daze. The explosive force of a shell had exploded his ear drums and lung tissue. John Wood grabbed him and threw him underneath a tank and between its tracks, then crawled in after him. The tank driver, seeing what had transpired, opened the hatch door and accommodatingly threw them a blanket. Then he closed the door again.

William P. Kelly became something of a hero to our company after the war. He was sent to a hospital in Paris to recover from his wounds. One day, after we had been transferred from Austria to Heddesheim in western Germany, Kelly shocked everybody by walking into the company orderly room. He had gone AWOL (absent without leave) from the Hospital in Paris and had hitchhiked back to Germany to find us. The captain was elated that one of his men would do this and, I am sure, took care of any problems about Kelly's absence from the hospital.[3] We hear much about "bonding" these days, but this incident illustrates the bonding that takes place among men, especially infantrymen, who have gone through a deadly experience together.

When the shelling began the men on the road scattered out to avoid concentration in one spot. This included Pop Davis. A shell exploded in a tree above him and a piece of shrapnel, with its terrible force, entered his back. When the other men came to him, he looked up and quietly said, "I can't get my breath." That was all. He died a few moments later. He was always quiet and soft-spoken.

For many years I reflected on the circumstances of that evening. I escaped the worst of the shelling because our squad was ordered to do something that none of us, I am sure, really wanted to do. Perhaps it saved our lives; we shall never know. I learned not to think of other people as being "luckier" than I was, a lesson I have never forgotten.

The whole company reflected on Nelson R. "Pop" Davis. We did not have much time or opportunity in combat to talk about the mysteries of life, such things as fate, predestination, accidents, chance, providence, or even theology. Perhaps the answers to these things must await a future day. I remember that one of the sergeants who had urged Pop to go back and ride in one of the vehicles said aloud, "If Pop had only done what we said, he would be alive with the rest of us."

We got across the Salzach River that night. Perhaps that was the night engineer assault boats took us part way and we waded the remaining distance in water waist deep. I only vaguely remember the actual crossing. It has faded away, overwhelmed by the events preceding it.

Part IV

Austria

Chapter 25

Arrival in an Austrian Village

(A "Friend" from California)

*"Blessed are the merciful: for they
shall obtain mercy."*
—Matthew 5:7

It was a bright warm day when we rolled into an Austrian village, riding on tanks and armored vehicles. The countryside, not far from the *Obertrumersee* north of Salzburg, possessed a grandeur that was a new experience for many of us: green hills and forests, pasture land and meadows, and high mountain peaks in the distance. Deer could be seen loping in and out of the wooded areas, and tiny farm villages nestled on the slopes and hillsides.

We had received orders during those last few days not to fire our rifles unless fired upon. Nor had we been taking any prisoners. Just waving them to the rear, as we met German soldiers straggling back from somewhere to the east.

As we sat in that beautiful village, waiting and wondering what next, Sergeant Eugene H. Walker, our company first-sergeant, came up to the tank on which I was riding and said, "Hatch, come into this house with me. There's a friend of yours in here."

I was puzzled at such a request—in a strange land during war time and thousands of miles from home. I climbed down from the tank and walked into the house with the sergeant. There in the vestibule stood two German soldiers.

"This man's from California," Sgt. Walker said, pointing to one of the German soldiers,. "Are you from California?" I asked, and he replied "Yes."

The German soldier then explained that he had lived and worked in California for about twelve years, including employment on the Hearst Ranch at San Simeon. During that time he became an American citizen. He returned to Germany in the late 1930s to get married and was drafted into the German army. He showed us pictures of his wife and two little children, and a letter from the American consul in Stuttgart, verifying his U.S. citizenship.

All this, obviously, had been to no avail.

Sgt. Walker then asked the two men where their military unit was and one replied that it had disintegrated and scattered. So they were just trying to make their way home. That was somewhere in Germany to the west, but they did not tell us where.

We visited for a few minutes, sharing memories of California. Finally Sgt. Walker looked at the two men and much to my surprise asked, "Why don't you fellows just take off those uniforms and go home?"

Our German friend explained that they had nothing else to wear. Their uniforms were wool and warm and they would need them for the long walk home. So we told them goodbye as they went out of the village, headed west toward home. I watched them for a moment and then went back to the tank on which I had been riding.

I thought I knew our company first-sergeant, but that day I learned that really I had never known him. There was mercy in his character, a quality I had failed to recognize and a quality often forgotten in time of war. To my dying day I shall remember his compassion toward those two men. I realized that he had a heart, and he knew the heart of the common soldier in any uniform. In thinking back on that moment, Jesus' words in the Sermon on the Mount come to mind: "Blessed are the merciful: for they shall obtain mercy."[1]

We remained in that tiny farm village, nestled on the hillside, for several days before moving to another one. Our time there had a pleasant beginning—I met a "friend" from California—and it had a pleasant ending, for there on May 8, 1945, my wife, Jo's, birthday, we received word that the war in Europe had come to an end.

Aboard the USS General Brooks crossing the Atlantic, homeward bound, June 1945

Chapter 26

The Old Mill and the Miller

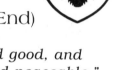

(A Good Place for Combat to End)

"And [we] found fat pasture and good, and the land was wide, and quiet, and peaceable."
—I Chronicles 4:40

"Sid, the captain says we are to go out this afternoon and see if there are any German soldiers in the houses around here. If we find anyone who looks like he might have been eligible for military service, we are to bring him in for questioning."

It was with these orders that Johnnie Jernigan our squad leader came to me one afternoon in Austria. We had been in the small village near the *Obertrumersee* only a few days, not more than a week, when we were loaded onto trucks and taken to another village some distance away. For what reason, most of us did not know, but there was always "The army reason."

It was with these orders that the two of us, Johnnie and I, armed with our rifles, set out over the beautiful Austrian hills. Since the war had officially ended, it was a mission we did not relish. But ours was not to reason why.

We hardly started on our search when Johnnie said to

me, "I want to show you something, something I saw yesterday." By the way he spoke, I sensed that it had little to do with military matters. My curiosity was aroused.

We walked over a low hill and down the other side. There by a stream of water was a scene I have never forgotten—everything about it was covered or blanketed with white. It was an old-fashioned flour mill grinding out the grain, the type of structure and operation that must have gone back for several centuries.

There was a large creaking wheel being turned by the water in the stream, the small building adjacent to the stream, and the miller going about his task. Everything, including the miller from head to toe, was covered by the white powder produced by grinding of the grain.

"Look at that," Johnnie exclaimed and we gazed on this old-world sight before us with interest and admiration. As we conversed briefly, the miller went about his business with never so much as a glance in our direction. Obviously, his task of grinding out the grain was not to be disturbed by the presence of foreign soldiers.

After a little while Johnnie said, "Let's go," and we started on our way to search for any members of the *Wehrmacht* who had taken refuge in the homes or cottages in the hills. We went to several places and received assurances that no one there had been in the military service.

Finally we came to a small cottage and knocked on the door. An older couple responded to our knock, and between them stood a teen-age young man, perhaps about fourteen years of age. I surmised that the man and woman were his grandparents, or perhaps they had been blessed with a son in middle age.

Since Johnnie spoke no German, it fell to my lot to attempt the inquiries. If the boy had been in military service, as had been so many of the young men, we would have to take him with us for questioning.

The older couple instantly became alarmed and assured us that the boy standing between them had not been in the German army. Every one of my inquiries brought a vehement denial that he had been a soldier.

We listened intently to the pleas of the boy's parents (or grandparents), trying to decide if they were telling the truth. At the same time we watched the bearing of the boy standing between them. He appeared to have nothing to hide. It became a real struggle in our own hearts as to our decision so we held a little discussion between ourselves.

Finally I said, "Let's not take him in." As squad leader, Johnnie had one more stripe than I did, but I knew I did not want to tear that boy away from his home. "Okay," Johnnie said and I think he was glad to let me decide.

It was a relieved couple that heard our decision. As we walked back to the village, it was Johnnie who had to report to Captain Hensley, the company commander. "I'll tell the captain, no German soldiers," he said.

The next day was Sunday. Except for the church bells ringing, everything was quiet in the village. Also, happily, there was no "busy work" for the soldiers.

In the afternoon children were playing and talking in the open area in the center of the village. Several of our men went out and visited with them. When they returned, they remarked, "The children say this is the village where the Christmas carol, 'Silent Night,' originated."

We took the children at their word. Sadly I did not think to ask them the name of the village. That oversight I have always regretted.

Three men and three villages may be said to have been involved in the creation and introduction of "Silent Night,

Holy Night" to the world. Joseph Mohr of Oberndorf wrote the words, Franz Gruber of Arnsdorf composed the music. A year later Fritz Mauracher, the organ repair man from Zillerthal, begged Gruber to give him a copy of the music so that he might introduce it to his village.[1] Which of the three villages we were in I do not know.

In a day or two we departed Austria for western Germany. That small village in the Austrian Tyrol was, for me, a good place for combat to end. I carry in my memory the picture of the old mill and the miller, the aged parents pleading for their son; the church bells on Sunday, and the message of the children. It was a place "quiet, and peaceable."

Our relief and delight at what we found in Austria can be appreciated even more if I mention briefly the military strategy which had been planned for us. It had been rumored that the Germans might make a last stand in the Alps Mountains of southern Germany and Austria. The area included Hitler's retreat at Berchtesgaden and supposedly would be an "impregnable fortress" capable of holding out for two years. It became known as "the Redoubt." The assignment for the 86th Division was to drive through the heart of Bavaria and fight its way into Austria which would mean attacking the Redoubt. We may be thankful that this so-called Redoubt never materialized.[2]

Part V

A Pause for Reflections

Chapter 27

"Haben Sie Eier?"
("Have You Any Eggs?" Reflections on Eating During Combat)

"Thou shalt eat the herb of the field."
—Genesis 3:18.

For some time during combat I experienced a longing for fresh vegetables. It occurred to me one day as we hiked through a grassy field that I might find some greens to eat. I didn't see anything that I recognized, mustard greens for example, so I finally pulled some tender shoots of green grass and chewed on them. The taste was strong, and I spit out the juice, but I received a measure of satisfaction from just trying.

We ate well in combat. In the streets of Cologne the cooks set up a field kitchen and served us hot meals. (When German artillery came over, we ducked into a doorway.) Most of the time it was the familiar "C" and "K" rations.

Early on in combat we realized there was food around for the taking. To a certain extent we fell back on the ancient art of foraging—something I understand armies have done for millennia. This was not because we were hungry; we simply wanted a change of fare.

When we pulled back from Cologne we found ourselves

in a rural farming area. A couple of the men with farming experience liberated a small pig, butchered it and ate it. This, however, created an incident of international dimension and these fellows were ordered by our officers to pay the farmer for his pig.

Another instance—cruder and more comical—concerned a goose. One of my buddies cast covetous eyes on the lovely creature. He captured it, killed it, and dressed it in the cellar of the house where he was staying. He then attempted to dispose of the evidence—blood, feathers, and all. After that he boiled it on the stove. This process went on all afternoon, but still the goose was too tough to eat.

When the German woman returned to her house, now occupied by American soldiers, she noticed her lovely goose was missing and her suspicions were aroused. After much evasion and equivocation, the G.I. confessed to his crime and made amends. But this did not bring back the precious goose.

One night about ten o'clock while advancing through a small town, the order came to halt. The people, leaning on their window sills, had been quietly watching us. At that moment I got what I thought was a brilliant idea. Turning to an older couple in the open window, I asked, *"Bitte, haben Sie Brot und Marmalade?"*[1] "Please, do you have any bread and jam?"

While the husband remained at the window casually smoking his pipe, the lady of the house went to her kitchen and returned immediately with a large round loaf of bread. Holding it against herself, she skilfully carved off a large slice, smeared something white on it, and handed it to me. I ate it with relish. She then gave several other men a slice of her delicious *"Brot und Marmalade."* We engaged in a few minutes of conversation and then the line of soldiers began to move.

Since that time I have always liked the heavy European bread. Jesus' words, "I am the bread of life,"[2] are more meaningful to me now. Old world bread must have always been substantial food.

On another occasion late at night two of us ventured into the cellar of a German home. There we saw jars of canned peaches. We took one of them, opened it and sampled the fruit. It had no flavor so we put the jar back on the shelf. When I returned home from Europe I was told that it was probably canned without sugar.

"*Haben Sie Eier?*" "Do you have any eggs?" This was a phrase every G.I. knew. The morning before we advanced on Ingolstadt, I heard a knock on the door of the house where we had been billeted for the night, followed by the familiar call, "*Haben Sie Eier?*" As the German family went to the door, I called out over their heads, "We've already asked for their eggs." "Oh, okay," my fellow American said and went on. It was simply a case of respecting somebody else's territory.

One experience has always remained for me a pleasant memory, despite the bitter cold wind that brought it about.

Spring supposedly had come to Bavaria and we had turned in our heavy winter overcoats. But that night, as we advanced on foot across an open plain, the wind, mixed with a few snowflakes, literally howled. We had only our raincoats to put on over our other clothing. I lay flat on the ground, and even down in a ditch by the side of the road, in an effort to escape the cold.

About four in the morning I spotted a farmhouse in the distance and decided it should be checked out—and perhaps it would provide an opportunity to get warm. Two of us went up to the house and I shouted toward a second-floor window. A woman and then a man put their heads out. "We are Americans; are there any German soldiers in there?" I asked. "Nein, *nein*," they both said. "May we come in and get warm?" I then asked and they responded in the affirmative.

Several of us went into the kitchen and soon Lieutenant Keeton and half our platoon had crowded in, sitting on the bench that went around the kitchen wall. A warm fire was burning in the stove and for the next hour our hosts, however reluctantly, cooked eggs and served them to us. Many of the fellows, having eaten, went sound to sleep sitting on that bench and leaning on each other.

Lieutenant Keeton remained very much awake during our Bavarian country breakfast. I was sitting across the kitchen from him and at one point I noticed him talking quietly to the soldier next to him. Then they reached in their pockets, took out their billfolds, and pulled out some paper currency. I do not recall now what kind of money we were carrying, but whatever it was, our platoon took up a collection and handed it to the German woman. She very graciously thanked the lieutenant, although over the years I have feared that it would be a long time before her chickens caught up with the number of eggs we devoured.

A similar incident about ten days later ended quite differently. We entered a small village on tanks and armored vehicles. It was Kirchdorf near the town of Haag. Again we crowded into a kitchen, sat on the bench around the wall, and again we were being fed generously. This time an elderly grandmother was supervising the whole procedure. Unfortunately, a couple of the fellows got noisy—to the embarrassment, I believe, of some of the others.

In the midst of this scene two young Germans, apparently lower ranking officers, walked into the kitchen. They went directly to the grandmother who was standing in front of where I was sitting, bowed politely and thanked her, and then told her goodbye. When she asked where they were going, they replied, "We must go with the Americans." Then they turned and walked out, with hardly a glance at any of us.

Outside the window I could see a platoon of German soldiers marching up the road. Their boyish faces told me right away that they were teen-agers, perhaps the troops commanded by the two young officers. I surmised that they would not complete their surrender until they came into the kitchen and thanked the grandmother. I must say that I was impressed.

We stayed in Kirchdorf for two or three days. While there the principal topic of conversation among the men was the little church about one hundred yards up the road. Many of them walked up to see it and marvelled at its beautiful interior. Moments like that lifted us above the experiences of war and reminded us that there was another way of life to which, God willing, we could all return.

Our time in Kirchdorf was our last duty with General Patton's Third Army. When we left there and proceeded into Austria we became members of the Seventh Army.[3]

I have been writing about eating, but what about drinking, was there any of that? Not as much as one might think, war stories to the contrary notwithstanding. A drunken soldier was a menace to his buddies and the officers could not tolerate that. I have mentioned in an earlier chapter ("My Ambulance to Bavaria") how one of our fellows was intoxicated when we loaded onto the trucks in Hohenlimburg, preparatory to going to Bavaria.

One incident, also in Hohenlimburg, included a lesson for us. "Chief," as everyone called him, was a young American Indian boy in one of the other platoons. He came one night to the house we had occupied, apparently drunk, and pounded on the door, demanding to be let in. Lieutenant Keeton shouted at us not to let him in and to get away from the door. Chief might fire his rifle through the door. When we refused him admittance and told him to go away, he spoke back to us in firm and sober tones, "Don't call me Chief, don't call me Chief." It had never occurred to us that his nickname offended him. It was a lesson for us in racial sensitivity in a day when not much thought was given to it.

In regard to drinking, another incident was much more pleasant. On one of those days when we were riding on tanks through Bavaria we came to a community where the men discovered a large soft-drink factory. Quite a few of them enjoyed a bottle of pop as they stood in the front yard of the building, and even the German proprietors and employees seemed amused by the whole situation. They stood out on the lawn in front of the building, laughing and smiling. The tank on which I was riding also stopped for a few minutes and those who wanted a drink of German soda pop ran in and got it.

This incident occurred while we were attached to General Patton's Third Army. I don't suppose the history books will attribute any of the Third Army's success to our refreshing pause at the soft drink factory.

Foraging as we did, I am sure we ate the people's food in a time when food would soon become scarce, if not already so. One of our young men who realized this was Fred Eckhardt, a boy of German background from Edgerton, Wisconsin. Fred was exceptional in our company in that his father had served in the German army in World War I and had earned the Iron Cross. Fred was proud of this and openly mentioned it to us or to German civilians with whom he might be having conversation. He told how his parents, faced with star-

Fred Eckhardt

vation conditions in Germany, emigrated to America in the early 1920s.

At the beginning of our aggressive combat in the Ruhr Pocket fighting, a small village was one of our first objectives. "F" Company was to move in ahead of us and we were to follow. We were situated on high ground overlooking the village with "F" Company to our right. We watched as they set up machine guns and fired into the village. Their tracer bullets, in the dusk of early evening made a spectacular display but set nearly every house on fire.

It was an appalling sight as the flames went high into the air. The people, ignoring us on the high ground, walked slowly back from the woods nearby and watched their houses burn. The cows remained undisturbed as they grazed in the field nearby.

We slept on the ground in the village that night. In one

of the few remaining structures the men found sausages and meat hanging from the rafters and helped themselves. Fred, however, commented to me that this was the people's food supply for the winter. Now they would have little to eat.

Our foraging finally came to a halt in Austria. Safely settled in the little village near the Obertrumersee, we received the news that the war was officially over. To celebrate the occasion, some of the men went hunting. They soon bagged a deer which were plentiful in the area. Amidst great excitement they brought it to the house where we were staying, butchered it, and cooked portions of it, sharing it with everybody. Unfortunately the meat was very tough. We ate it anyway.

Hardly had this feat been accomplished when the order swiftly came down, "No more hunting! The people depend on the wild game for their food supply." From then on it was army chow.

A few weeks later, in the town of Heddesheim in western Germany, the cooks were giving the remaining food after meals to the German children. The children came with large tin cans equipped with wire handles and waited patiently until the American soldiers had been fed. Hunger, I fear, had already come to Germany and the food the children received was small and insufficient compensation for the pig, the goose, the countless eggs, the sausages, the venison and even the *"Brot und Marmalade"* that the conquering armies had consumed.

Here someone may enjoy challenging me: "What about the tender shoots of green grass that you chewed on?" Let us not treat the grass too lightly. Did not God say to the first man, "Thou shalt eat the herb of the field"? In the Hebrew text of Scripture, the word for "herb" means "greens" in the sense of food for men."[4] If I had known more about botany—specifically, greens and herbs—we might have had a salad that day.

Chapter 28

Ol' Iry from West Virginia
(The Man from Strange Creek)

"The steps of a good man are ordered by theLORD."
—Psalm 37:23

Sergeant Fillmore (not his real name) was about to commit one of the unpardonable sins of army life—bucking the chow line—when things turned into push and shove.

In the process Private First Class Ira Young was knocked to the ground. Not for long however, for he came up flying, with arms flailing, and his mess gear hit Sergeant Fillmore alongside the head. Now it was the sergeant's turn to go down. At this point cooler heads prevailed.

"Young, you're not supposed to hit a non-commissioned officer," the lieutenant said with a faint smile on his face and a twinkle in his eye. "We'll have to take your stripe away."

Ira Young had been private first class for one day. He had one stripe sewn on his fatigue jacket; the other was supposed to come later when he had more time. Now he needn't bother.

To the men in Company "E," Ira Young was "Ol' Iry" from Strange Creek, West Virginia." Ask him where he was from and he never said "West Virginia." It was just "Strange

From left: Cpl. Elmer P. Brown, Phil McLain, Pvt. Ira Young

Creek." If someone asked, "Where's that?" he replied disgustedly, "Strange Creek."

Ira was one of fifteen children, nine of whom survived to adulthood. One time I asked, "Iry, where did you fit in?" and he replied, "Right in the middle."

As a teenager, Ira joined the C.C.C., the Civilian Conservation Corps of the Roosevelt era. From there he went into the army and was sent to Camp Atterbury, Indiana, where the army helped young recruits improve their reading and writing. When it became evident that Ira really did know his ABC's he was sent to the 86th Infantry Division.

The 86th "Blackhawk" Division, by the time it was sent overseas, was composed primarily of young men from two sources, the college campus and the Army Air Corps. Congress had recently eliminated the A.S.T.P. (Army Specialized Training Program), which deferred college students. The army itself had decided it had enough pilots and airmen for the time being so men in the process of training were sent to the ground forces where they were needed.[1]

"How'd I git in with these college boys?" Ira used to exclaim. His lack of academic achievement did not prevent his becoming one of the company's "mighty men of valour," a man of renown.[2]

"I'm stout as a mule" was one of Ira's favorite expressions. It was not an idle boast for one day at Camp Livingston, Louisiana, he backed up to a jeep, put his hands under the bumper, and lifted the vehicle off the ground. Captain Charles C. Lantis from San Francisco, California, company commander at the time, witnessed Ira's feat of strength and said, "I want you to report to the motor pool in the morning." There Ira spent the rest of his time in Company "E."

During our time at Camp San Luis Obispo, California, we took various types of amphibious training at the Navy base at Morro Bay. One day the engineers gave Ira a crane to drive and told him to take off. He proceeded down the main street of the town of Morro Bay with the boom straight up in the air, ripping out wires as he went. For a time Morro Bay, California, was out of communication with the rest of the world.[3]

The only time Ira's popularity was endangered was when some of the men complained about the food. A high ranking officer came to the company and conducted a survey. When he sought Ira's opinion, the man from Strange Creek replied, "Best food I ever et." Ira's buddies were enraged, the cooks were vindicated, and the campaign for "better chow" collapsed.

In those army days, Ira chewed tobacco. He introduced

this quaint art to one of the college boys and rumor had it that the two of them had used their tobacco as a weapon at close range. This, I assure my readers, was Ira's only war-time atrocity.

While in combat Ira drove the truck that delivered rations to us at the front. But the so-called front was a shifting proposition and on one occasion he could not make the return trip with the truck load of rations. The Germans had come between us and Ira and he was thwarted at every turn. "You can't go through there," the G.I.s told him at the road-blocks. "They'll capture you."

For three days we saw and heard nothing from Ira. For three days and nights we engaged in combat with nothing to eat. One night as we moved toward a German position we came upon an American ration truck. Its contents were dumped in the road. "Don't touch 'em," those in the lead shouted back to us, "they may be booby-trapped." And so we left them in the road. In the meantime, at home in West Virginia, a telegram arrived saying that Pvt. Ira Young was "missing in action."

One morning Ira arrived unexpectedly and there was rejoicing in the company. We were strung out along a road for several hundred yards. A jeep drove down the line loaded with cans of "C" rations. Captain Hensley was sitting in the back and as the jeep went along he literally tossed cans of rations to us—two cans to a man. I shall never forget how my arms involuntarily went into the air to catch the cans tossed to me.

Ol' Iry never went to town on a pass during those days in Company "E." He had never ridden a city bus and did not want to try. He gave his pass privileges to his buddies in the motor pool, especially Phil McLain, one of the college boys, who hailed from Miami, Florida.

In the years following the war Phil became the Reverend Phil McLain. In the early 1980s he felt a burden to locate Ira Young. On a trip through West Virginia he went to Strange Creek and was told, "Ira Young is dead." Later he learned that it was Ira's father, not the Ira Young of World War II days. He obtained enough information to trace the younger Ira to White Sulphur Springs, West Virginia. I still remember the letter from Phil which said in effect, "I have found Ira Young."

Today Ira and his wife Doris live in a beautiful two-story mansion on a hilltop overlooking Highway 92 in West Virginia. It was there that several of us held a 1990 reunion. Ira's holdings were spread out before him in the valley below—country store, automobile dealership, rental properties, and a cable television service. There would be no television up and down that valley if it were not for Ira Young, entrepreneur.

Ol' Iry was the nearest thing we had in our company to the famous "Willie and Joe" of World War II days. These were the characters through whom cartoonist Bill Mauldin lifted the spirits of the ground troops, especially the infantrymen.[4]

Now a successful and well-liked business man in his community, some would say it could only happen in the U.S.A. Ira had some things going for him, including a Godly mother at home during the war years, and soon after the war a Christian wife.

Ira and Doris have been blessed with four lovely daughters and now a host of grandchildren. Their only son died in a tragic automobile accident several years ago. In the living room of their home hangs a beautiful painting of Jesus and two of His disciples on the walk to Emmaus.[5] Underneath the painting is a plaque: "To Ira and Doris Young, in memory of Your Son, Robert Ira Young. From your Friends in Company E, 342nd Infantry Regiment, 86th Division."

Ira Young—to us always, the man from Strange Creek—has known poverty and wealth, joy and sorrow, and war and peace. Perhaps something else must be taken into consideration. The psalmist says, "The steps of a good man are ordered by the LORD: and he delighteth in his way. Though he fall, he shall not be utterly cast down: for the LORD upholdeth him with his hand."[6]

In 1993 my wife and I went to West Virginia again to visit Ira and Doris. They took us to Strange Creek and showed us the little house on the knoll. On the last Sunday with them they took us to the buffet at the golf course at the world famous Greenbriar Hotel.

It was a sumptuous affair that day. A party of about thirty of us, Ira's children and grandchildren, gathered around a large circular table. Needless to say, we ate like kings. After the lunch we went for a walk out on the beautiful golf course where, we were told, President Eisenhower used to play. "Iry," I said, "you did not keep us waiting today for our rations. And there was no Sergeant trying to break into

Sunday buffet at the Greenbrier Hotel. From left: Doris and Ira Young, Sid and Jo Hatch

the chow line."

I have reflected many times on Ira Young. Although faithful and well-liked by his fellow soldiers, for some reason he never received that one stripe which would have made him private-first-class in the army. In civilian life, through perseverance and hard work, he became citizen-first-class. There are many men and women who have served their country humbly and inconspicuously in the military during time of war, and in time of peace have gone on to become leaders in their community and field of endeavor. Such a person was Ira Young.

From left: Ira Young, John Wood, Sid Hatch, 1991

Part VI

Heddesheim

Chapter 29

Return to Heddesheim

"The recollection of good people is a blessing."
—Proverbs 10:7.[1]

On my desk is a small black book. The title on the cover, printed with gold leaf and in quaint old-fashioned type, is: *Neues Testament und Psalmen.* Inside on the flyleaf are these words: *"für Erinnerung an Ihre Zeit in Heddesheim bei Mannheim. Fam. Gustner. 22, Mai 1945"* (for remembrance of Your Time in Heddesheim by Mannheim. Family Gustner. May 22, 1945).

The end of the war in Europe, May 8, 1945, found us in the beautiful Austrian countryside north of Salzburg. We did not remain there long, leaving early one morning before daybreak and heading west, we knew not where.

Our convoy traveled along a hillside overlooking the city of Salzburg. The sight of Salzburg at sunrise was a scene I shall never forget. The Salzach River flowed through the city. The ancient buildings, the great cathedral, and the mighty castle on the hill, were outlined in the morning twilight. In the sky to the east were those reddish streaks of light which the Psalmist has called "the wings of the dawn."[2] But we could not contemplate the scene for long. It was only the beginning of a long and wearisome journey and our convoy soon left Salzburg far behind.

We rode all day and into the night, passing through scenes of devastation along the way. It was long after midnight when we arrived in a small community in western Germany

Heddesheim, near Mannheim, 1945

and there, in the middle of the night, our convoy stopped.

"Two men to each house," someone shouted, and Johnnie Jernigan and I, half-asleep, were taken into one of the homes. A German woman met us and showed us to our room. There for the next several hours we slept off the rigors of the trip.

We remained in that village seventeen days,[3] and although we were foreign troops billeted in their homes, the people treated us courteously. There was some military duty, time for a pass to Heidelberg, religious services in the nearby *Evangelische Kirche,* and moments of happiness and sadness all mixed together, which reminded us that a time of terrible strife had just come to an end.

One day shouts rang out in the village street. We went out to see what the commotion was. People were running to the edge of the village and gazing across the open plain. There in the distance, like silhouettes against the landscape, several figures moved slowly in our direction. We soon were able to distinguish soldiers in gray uniforms.

The group of people at the edge of the village was composed mostly of women and children. As the men in the distance came closer, several of the women screamed and a little child, obviously frightened, began to cry. Then several people broke away from the crowd and ran to meet the men, who were plainly tired and weary and who had walked from heaven knows where. There was no band to greet these men in gray, no village officials. But loved ones were there, and that is probably all they cared about. I watched for a little while and then turned and walked away. It was their moment of joy, the only consolation they had.

The family circle in the home where Johnnie and I stayed consisted of four people, Maria the mother, her two children, Emie and Lisela, and Maria's brother Peter. Peter was a German soldier who, somehow had gotten home from the war. We asked no questions. Maria's husband was away in the Wehrmacht, but she knew not where, or if he would ever come home.

The days in the village passed quickly and we wondered, are we going home from here, or will they send us directly to the Far East? Finally the news came: home first and then the Pacific.

Our duffel bags were packed and in the street. From here we were to go to a nearby railroad station, climb on freight cars, and travel back to Camp Old Gold in France. It was *"Auf Wiedersehen"* to Heddesheim.

I looked at my duffel bag. There on top was a small bouquet of wild flowers from the field nearby, and a slip of paper with a name on it, *"Fam. Jöst,"* and the address on Friedrichstrasze. The message was obvious.

Time does fly and in 1980 our oldest son David entered the army as a dentist. He was assigned to a base in Germany not far from Bayreuth. In 1983, as parents are prone to do, my wife and I went to visit him and his family.

The time there in Germany was an opportunity to see as a tourist what I had once seen as a soldier. Occasionally I would think of the village and the experiences of 1945, and wonder if I should say anything.

As the time of our visit drew to a close, I realized that a once-in-a-lifetime opportunity was about to pass away. "David," I commented one day, "if we can go back to that village in western Germany, I believe I can find the street and the family. If they are still there."

"Don't worry," he replied, "Germans don't move."

It's several hundred kilometers from the village of Kirchenthumbach near Bayreuth to the Mannheim area. Finally on the autobahn we saw the sign, *Heddesheim.*

But this was no village! It was a town, a small city, a suburb of larger cities. We hunted for an hour and finally a young German boy, tinkering on his car, told us the location of Friedrichstrasse.

I did not recognize where we were. The field where we had gathered as an infantry company was gone. The open plain across which the men in gray had trudged was now covered, block after block, with streets and beautiful new apartments and condominiums. Hope was fast turning into hopelessness.

David dared to knock at the front entrance of one of the attractive dwellings. A lady came to the door and eyed us cautiously. When he explained the innocent nature of our mission, she said, "There's an elderly lady and her daughter who live down the street in that direction," and she pointed toward the old district of Heddesheim.

As we walked in that direction, some of the houses began to take on a familiar look, even though most of them had been remodeled. Finally we came to one which had been remodeled into a two-story duplex. The name was by the door. This was it.

David rang the doorbell and I stood there wondering what to expect. My wife waited across the street, camera in hand, to watch the proceedings. A middle-aged woman looked out from the second floor window. David, fluent in German, explained who we were and what we wanted. A different look came over her face—I did not know how to interpret it—and she disappeared from the window. We stood at the door, still wondering.

From left: Maria Jöst; Sid Hatch; Maria's daughter, Emie

In a few moments the front door opened and two women stood there. One was the woman who had looked out the window, the other was a lady with snow white hair. I looked at them, still not sure.

"Are you Maria Jöst?" I asked the elderly woman in German. She did not say anything, but rather, with the younger woman's help, stepped forward and kissed me on the cheek. It had been over thirty-eight years, but I knew we had found the right place.

We visited for the next two hours, and the refreshments were simple, cookies and a soft drink. "I don't drink," Maria explained later during the course of the evening. "That's why I am still here."

"Are you Catholics?" Maria asked, and I explained we were evangelicals. It does not matter," she said, "you are Christians."

"Sid, you never wrote," Maria said. I remembered the little bouquet on my duffel bag, and the slip of paper with the family name and address. I winced, but offered no excuses.

Then there came time for the hard questions. "Where is Peter?" I asked. "Peter is dead," she replied.

I remembered the men in gray trudging across the open field, and wondered if I dared to ask, but finally did. "Maria, did your husband come home? Did he return from the war?"

"Yes," she replied, "but he died in 1967." I suspected, but did not ask, that his war experiences had left him an exhausted and broken man.

After touring the remodeled home and meeting Emie's husband in the upstairs apartment, the time came to leave. The day's drive and the emotion of the evening had left us all very tired. As we said good-bye, Emie exclaimed, "*Mutter ist fertig!*" which, in the light of the circumstances and freely translated, meant, "Mother is at the end of her rope! She is exhausted."

During the course of the evening Maria had said that we must return to Germany for her 85th birthday which was not far away. All I could say was, "We'll try."

Maria never reached her 85th birthday. It was hardly more than a year later when the sad news came. She had had a stroke, and soon after that she died.

I look occasionally at the little black New Testament and Psalms on my desk. One of Maria's neighbors gave it to me, the Gustner family. It reminds me of the Christians I met in Heddesheim.

Yes, I do read it once in a while. It's a revision of Luther's translation of the Scriptures. The language is different, but the message is the same.

War leaves us with many experiences and many memories, some good, some bad. However, God can give us inner strength to be selective in what we remember. "Whatsoever things are lovely, whatsoever things are of good report ... think on these things.[4] This is the exhortation of the apostle Paul, and it is the way I feel about the days in Heddesheim.

Chapter 30

A Day We Laid Our Rifles Down

(A Parable of the Future)

"Nation shall not lift up sword against nation, neither shall they learn war any more."
—Isaiah 2:4.

In writing these memoirs one experience remains different from the others. It has become for me a parable of the last days and the age to come.

We had hardly settled down in the village near the Obertrumersee when an order came: "Turn in your ammunition." Its suddenness and unexpected nature took us by surprise. It was prompted, however, by an unfortunate accident.

Three of the men were sitting against an old barn cleaning their equipment when one of them accidentally discharged his rifle. The bullet pierced the thigh of the man next to him and in some freakish way grazed the skull of the third soldier. Both men were taken away in an army ambulance and we did not see them again.

Although it was readily available in case of emergency, to give up our ammunition left us feeling somewhat disarmed and vulnerable. It was very much a part of our lives and equipment. We did however continue to carry our rifles.

In western Germany in the peaceful community of Heddesheim we still carried our rifles everywhere we went, even on pass to Heidelberg. A moment came, however, when we laid our rifles down.

On a quiet Sunday morning word went about the area that Protestant services for the men in our battalion would be conducted in the afternoon at the local *Evangelische Kirche*. Chaplain Gerald T. Krohn would be presiding. Chaplain Krohn was one of the chaplains who had conducted the memorable service on board ship in the North Atlantic. Later, during an engagement in the Ruhr Pocket fighting, he distinguished himself by volunteering as a litter bearer to help evacuate the wounded.[1]

Chaplin Gerald T. Krohn

As I walked to the church several blocks from "our" house on Friedrichstrasze I met other men going in the same direction, so we joined ranks and walked along together. Upon entering the church we were greeted by the chaplain's assistant who was standing just inside the front door. "The German pastor asks that rifles not be carried into the sanctuary," he said. "You may leave them here in the foyer," and he pointed to a corner where several rifles had already been placed.

This request, which seemed more like an order, went against the grain and for an instant I flinched. Since when were we taking orders from a conquered foe—especially to give up our rifles?

But then with no outward hesitation I complied and we

all stacked our rifles in the corner. We went in and seated ourselves in the sanctuary.

About fifty G.I.s were present. Chaplain Krohn, tall and impressive, was standing in the center aisle. The German pastor was walking about at the side of the sanctuary, looking over in our direction. He was of medium height and pleasant appearance and dressed conservatively in a dark suit. He seemed well aware of what was occurring.

In a moment Chaplain Krohn made an announcement. With rather serious mien he said, "Men, the German pastor asks that rifles not be brought into the sanctuary. If any of you have your rifles with you, please take them out and place them in the foyer." Several men got up and went out. In a moment they returned and the service began.

We sang several hymns and the church organist, a young German woman, accompanied us. Then Chaplain Krohn preached. I must confess, I had some difficulty keeping my mind on the sermon. I had been sufficiently impacted already by the preliminaries and the circumstances.

After the service our German hosts extended to us an unusual gesture of Christian hospitality. While the organist played, at least a dozen men who remained at the church gathered around the organ and attempted to sing some hymns. It soon became obvious that our repertoires were different so she yielded the organ to the chaplain's assistant who was himself a qualified musician and the selection changed to familiar American hymns.

With the songfest the time at the *Evangelische Kirche* came to an end. It made a nice conclusion to the afternoon service.

I enjoyed that service so long ago at the German church in Heddesheim. But it has been the impact—perhaps shock— of the greeting at the door that has remained uppermost in my mind. Added to the German Pastor's request was the cooperation of the American chaplain.

It seemed strange to take orders from two Christian ministers to lay our rifles down—men from nations so recently at war with one another. Now that moment has taken on a prophetic significance, a parable of the future.

The prophet Isaiah tells us of a day when the nations will lay their weapons down. "...they shall beat their swords into plowshares, and their spears into pruninghooks; nation shall not lift up sword against nation, neither shall they learn war any more."[2]

As it was that afternoon in Heddesheim, perhaps this disarmament program will be implemented by the servants of that One whose title will be, "The Prince of peace."[3]

The apostle Paul assures us that we shall live and reign together with Christ.[4] He also calls us "ambassadors for Christ" to whom has been committed "the word of reconciliation."[5] These words have an evangelical charge now. In the age to come they will have a most literal fulfillment. As ambassadors of the King we shall carry His orders to the nations to beat their swords into plowshares.

The service at the German church in Heddesheim transcends the gulf that separates our age from the next one. God lets some things brood quietly in our heads and hearts that in years to come they may bring forth a spiritual message.

Chapter 31

The Impartiality of Suffering

"God is no respecter of persons: But in every nation he that feareth him ... is accepted with him."
—Acts 10:34-35.

We were walking down the street after the service at the German church when someone riding on a bicycle caught up with us. To our surprise, it was the church organist.

"Would you like to come to my home, meet my family and listen to some music?" she asked in German. This invitation was as surprising as the one inviting us to leave our rifles in the foyer of the church.

Our little procession of eight or ten men stopped and we looked at one another. Should we or should we not accept this invitation? An obvious feeling of reluctance swept over the group and an English-language discussion ensued. I think there was a feeling of fear and concern about the decorum involved—how should we conduct ourselves in such a situation?—and also the problem of fraternization, even though all of us were billeted in German Homes.

When the discussion ended, two of us had decided to go to the organist's home, I and one other soldier. My buddy in this new venture was Fred Eckhardt from Edgerton, Wisconsin. Because of his own German background, Fred always felt comfortable in a German home. With the decision made, we followed the organist while the other men went their way.

Upon arrival at the house a short distance from the church we were ushered in the front door and then ascended a narrow steep stairway. It was quite awkward for us as we attempted to make our way up the stairway with rifles slung over our shoulders and banging against the wall.

At the top of the stairway we entered a small but nicely furnished living room and were introduced to the family. The father was Herr Boertner and we were informed that he was the treasurer or financial secretary of the town of Heddesheim. His office was at the *Rathaus* or city hall, a building not far from the neighborhood in which we were billeted. Frau Boertner, a quiet woman, was seated next to him. Then there was the older sister who said very little and didn't seem to appreciate our presence. The organist had already identified herself as Maria.

With the formalities over, everyone was seated. Herr Boertner had only one leg. His left leg was severed at the hip and he got about with crutches. During the remainder of the afternoon he remained seated with Frau Boertner beside him. The family must have noticed that we observed the father's condition because they explained that he had lost his leg in the first World War. As combat veterans, we expressed our sympathy and also our comprehension of the tragedy of war. Frau Boertner smiled appreciatively, the older sister still saying very little.

Cookies and punch were served, we conversed for a few minutes and then Maria stood up. In a rather formal manner she announced that she was going to play a piece on the piano. This was her own composition and was in tribute to her husband. *"Für meinen Mann,"* she said, "And where was her Mann?" we asked. *"An der Ostfront,"* she replied.

"On the east front." These foreboding words augured the worst possible fate. We wondered if she fully realized the possible fate of her husband. But we tried not to reveal the thoughts going through our minds and simply listen to the music.

Maria's composition was long and quite beyond the musical comprehension of this soldier, but perhaps it was just as well. It gave us an opportunity to think about the circumstances. When she finished she stood up again and we expressed our thanks.

Fred and I glanced at each other. It was time to go. We thanked each one, slung our rifles over our shoulders and as gracefully as we could moved across the room to the stairway and made the descent to the street.

We did not say much as we walked back to our billets. The afternoon had contained enough surprises to keep us in thought for a while.

The time in the Boertner home impressed us again with the domestic tragedy of war. I went into combat in Germany mindful that my cousin, Harold Jobe of Covina, California, a young man with whom I had grown up, had perished in the hedgerows of Normandy. Cut down by machine gun fire, he lived only two minutes. His last words, according to one of his buddies, were, "Tell my parents not to cry." Now I had been reminded again that the gods of war are no respecters of persons, homes, or peoples. All alike suffer at their hands.

Our consolation is that the God of heaven is also no respecter of persons. If it is the common people who suffer in war, it is the common people to whom He has extended His love and affection. The apostle Paul tells us to look at our own ranks.[1] It is not the leading men of the earth whom God has called but the weak and humble. So also we have the assurance of Christ's Sermon on the Mount: "Blessed are the meek: for they shall inherit the earth."[2]

Epilogue: Part A

Wolzhausen: 1990

*"For ye are all children of God
by faith in Christ Jesus."*
—Galations 3:26.

On April 8, 1945, our pleasant interlude in the village of Wolzhausen came to an end. We climbed aboard a convoy of trucks which took us into combat in the Ruhr industrial area of Germany.

Seated across from me in the back of the truck on which I was riding were two members of our company with whom I was not acquainted. As the trucks drove away they laughed and told what they had done to the house in Wolzhausen where they had stayed. It was not life-threatening, but it was malevolent and destructive.

I was embarrassed. Their prank was not typical of the officers and men of our company. And there were the Christians in Wolzhausen. Then I rationalized: "I'm powerless to do anything about it. I'll probably never have to face these people again. Try to forget it." And forget it I did, for almost forty-five years.

In 1989 I penned a short version of my story of Wolzhausen and the Scripture mottoes on the wall of the home there.

Although it was not exactly Bible study, I decided to include it in an issue of the Bible study magazine which I have been writing for many years and mailing to friends and acquaintances.

A reader in Savannah, Georgia, wrote to me asking, "Why don't you send your story to the *Bürgermeister* of Wolzhausen?" It was a suggestion which had already been made to me by my wife and family.

I hesitated to do so; it seemed presumptuous and bold. Finally I yielded to the suggestion. In October of 1989 my story was dispatched to the Bürgermeister of Wolzhausen, Germany.

The weeks went by and then the months. One day an envelope arrived with German postage and the word "Wolzhausen" in the return address. I must admit to a certain nervousness as I opened the envelope. It was from a Gerhard Becker of Wolzhausen who was fourteen years of age when our company arrived there. Mr. Becker wrote to me as follows.

Gerhard Becker
(Wolzhausen)
Bornbachsweg 3

Wolzhausen, in the months
of November 1989 and
January 1990

3565 BREIDENBACH

Dear Mr. Hatch,

We have received your letter which has caused a pleasant surprise and vivid discussions in our village. Many things have been discussed, reminiscences were called up. And so we came about the name of a man - he deceased in the meantime - who had told us the story of the New Testament that he once had given as a present to an US soldier.

A woman of our village has reported me all that. The discussion about your letter was made easier since our mayor published your whole letter in the "Weekly paper for the municipality of Breidenbach". (Please, allow me an interjection in this context. On the first of July 1974, Wolzhausen and other villages around were taken together as a bigger municipality in the frame of an administrative reform).

Before I shall answer the actual message of your letter, I just want to describe the geography of our village. The brook running through the centre is called the Perf. This brook actually divides Wolzhausen into two parts. The Perf is an affluent of the river Lahn, which falls into the Rhine. The bridge that you have mentioned connects the two parts of the village. It is still in existence, a little bit modernized, however. The Eastern part of the village is distinguished by a stronger slope than the Western part, where streets run almost even, as the lay-out of those days shows.

But in the meantime, many things have changed.

Dear Mr. Hatch! In your letter you speak about a power station and a large building. It just deals with a transformer station; at its right side we have had the municipal administration (in those days with the mayor's and audit's offices). I'm sure that you had your headquarters there.

The large building must have been the brewery; as a result of the war, it was not in operation in those times. The building is made of brick without plaster.

The transformer station and the municipal administration were situated at the Eastern side of the Perf, while the brewery has been at the Western side. I still recall that the American soldiers had their meeting point at the brewery.

Please, Sir, allow another personal experience with the brewery in the times of US-occupation. I was a boy of 14 years (born in 1930) and had approached quite near to the field kitchen. An American soldier — I remember that he had his rifle slung — urged me to disappear. It must have been a guard, I think. And I had the feeling: this is your own country, and you have nothing to say!

The man who gave you the New Testament was Adam Krug, who died many years ago. His wife in those times died before him, and also his second wife died in times long past. They only had one child, a son. As I learned from the Chronicle of Wolzhausen, this son was injured at Schitomir in Russia.

-2-

He died in the field hospital of Troppau on February 22, 1944 and was buried in the cemetery of Wolzhausen.

Other details of your letter have caused irritations among the inhabitants of Wolzhausen.

You talk about people looking for their bed covers. Moreover, you mention a family that remained at the table in silence, but then you only mention the mother.

This brings up the question if you only think of these two persons, or were also other people in the house?

The family of Adam Krug belonged to our Darbystic congregation. And so I believe that the New Testament that you received as a present was the Elberfeld translation of the Bible.

Within the village, we also speculated about other families, however, most of them are dead. I think that these speculations are incredible, since—among other facts—the street where Mr. Krug used to live is characterized in part only by a trifling slope. The house, however, is situated at the Western side of the brook.

Almost 45 years have passed since these events, many things have changed. Since the monetary reform in 1948, more buildings have been erected than we used to have for hundreds of years before. The so-called German economic wonder has resulted in considerable changes.

But the memories of the terrible times of war have not faded within the brains of our elder people. So, please, let me give a short report of those days from my personal point of view. When the US-troops arrived, we asked ourselves: How will they behave, what will they do? Probably the national socialists would be punished, though many of them were nothing but members of this party and didn't do any harm. On the other hand, there was also a certain touch of curiosity in me. My belief in a German victory was destroyed, when I saw the condition of German troops coming back and later on the well-equipped Americans.

In those days numerous Wehrmachts-goods had been evacuated in rural districts, in order to protect them from the air attacks by the enemy. For this reason, big halls had been seized. In Wolzhausen, they stored covers and captured Russian military clothes as well as evacuated oils. Nobody knew, if the Americans would seize all these things. And so our mayor decided to distribute all covers before the US-soldiers marched in. The inhabitants of Wolzhausen also received the oils and the military clothes. The covers had been bundled up in bundles of 10 covers each. And so some people came and went back with a hundred covers!

In those days we recognized that the foreign soldiers collected comforters. However, I supposed that they collected mattresses.

Suddenly we heard that the people of Wolzhausen had protested against this procedure to the commanding officer.

He ordered that the covers had to be brought back to the municipal building and our people got back their Eider-down covers. Our family lived in a small house so that we remained unaffected by the American soldiers.

-3-

But I remember that I went to the municipal building too and brought away some of our Wehrmacht-covers.

Unanimously we think that the old man who devotedly asked for the permission to milk his cow was Heinrich Fuchs, who also died long ago. His daughter Anna Fuchs did not remember this event, but our chronicle told me that the family Fuchs had to clear its house in those days. She could also tell me other things. Heinrich Fuchs was also a brother in Jesus Christ. He and his family belong to the Darbystic congregation.

I suppose, you are perhaps interested in learning something about the spiritual life in our village. Here's something in brief:

In the frame of the reformation by Dr. Martin Luther, our district became protestant in the 16th century, which means in a moderate Lutheran expression. In the 80ies of the 19th century, we had a religious revival in Wolzhausen; many people became converted to Jesus Christ, as it also was the case again in the following years and decades. I really think that we live a vivid religious life here, but on the other hand we leave much to be desired.

After World War II, many Catholics came to Wolzhausen (refugees and expellees).

As a consequence of different doctrines, we have also had separations here. The priests of the national church did not understand the situation of the converted people. They behaved in a critical way. The consequence was the separation from the national protestant church and the creation of different Holy Communion congregations. Darbystic doctrines caused new separations within these new Communion congregations, which then were united together as "Free Protestant Communions". The protestant church then cared for their people and started with Bible classes. Within the national protestant church there were many communions to which I belong too. The interpretation of the Bible plays an important role here, while we still remain members of our national church. Furthermore, I am member of the YMCA.

In Wolzhausen we had the foundation of a Free Protestant Communion. The Darbystic congregation is also very strong, and moreover, we have the Bible-class circle of the national church. And we have brethren with Whitsun opinions. Catholic people must go to church in Breidenbach. The national protestant church and the Free Protestant Communions work together in the frame of an alliance. A Baptist Communion has been in St.-Niedereisenhausen, a village situated 3km south of Wolzhausen.

But now, let me come back to the times of the US-occupation. Nobody in Wolzhausen was hurt, and people told me that many soldiers behaved in a very friendly way — not like enemies. The houses that had been occupied, however, had been damaged considerably. In one house, the soldiers had cut off all circuit lines, in another one, excrements had been stored in preserving jars. There was one man who became so angry about this that he decided to report the names of all national socialists to the Americans. Later on, three inhabitants of Wolzhausen — not all of them were members of the National Socialist Party — had to report to the district's military government in Biedenkopf. But nobody was captured. If those people had been blackened by this man? I don't know.

There was one house where your unit left a German-English dictionary. We, the boys, took it and learned some English with its help.

Your unit was in Wolzhausen for some 3 or 4 days. When you left the village, we had no other occupation here. Many other villages around had been occupied for months!

While the US-troops were in Wolzhausen, many German soldiers rummaged in the forests around the village. German people thought that American soldiers were quite fearful. But, of course, there was no need for you to risk the lives of many soldiers. Our German soldiers were starved, they did not have the strength to fight any longer. Many of them were captured later on, others tried hard to get home to their families. We helped them as much as possible by giving them a bed for a night or by telling them names of unoccupied area. Everybody longed for the end of the war. When the final capitulation was signed on May 8, 1945, we felt sadness and pain. But what had happened to the Jews — terrible crimes against humanity! Or what about the subjunction of the Slavic people? God's judgement for the German people was inescapable. A judgement that was meant to be an appeal for penance and conversion, for the contemplation of God's will. For sure, there have been crimes to the Germans too, e.g. I think about numerous air attacks on open cities and people in the country. We could certainly put the question: Who is to blame for this? But nevertheless, it cannot curtail our own responsibility.

Let me say it again, 45 years have passed. For the Federal Republic of Germany this means the longest period of peace in the younger German history. Our state is estimated worldwide, and sometimes even feared. Friendships have been established between people of different nations, this seemed to be impossible before. I should especially mention the German-French reconciliation which is of great importance for the European prospering. And also the friendship with the United States of America is of considerable importance for our people. In a human sense, this is the basis for freedom and peace in Western Europe.

World affairs have also changed considerably. Just think about the latest developments in Eastern Germany. We may now experience that all over the world, people find their way to Jesus Christ. This is wonderful! In Western Europe this is not so often the case, and this is deplorable. Nevertheless, there are also people finding a way to a vivid belief, young people are prepared to cooperate in religious communions. And this is really a reason to be happy and thankful!

Jesus Christ is the Light in the world. Those who follow him, will not walk in darkness, but build their house on a stable base. So let us grow stronger in the faith of vivid hope. In this confidence, I send best wishes to you and our brethren in the United States, and it would be a pleasure to hear from you again.

Yours very truly,

sgd. Gerhard Becker

I have incorporated Mr. Becker's letter into this story with no editorial changes on my part. I want my readers to experience its feeling and emotion as I did when reading it for the first time.[1]

In the months that followed receipt of his letter, Mr. Becker and I engaged in a lengthy correspondence. His first letter had been in English, subsequent letters were in German. Our mutual Christian faith was able to heal the wounds of the past.

Later that year a miracle took place. Friends made it possible for me to return to Wolzhausen with my wife Jo and in the company of another couple, Paul and Dorothy Koch of Milwaukie, Oregon. For two days we were the guests of Gerhard and Dorothea Becker in their home. Our friends were received into the home of a neighbor, Frau Karin Kult and family.

The Beckers live in a comfortable bungalow style home, comparable to an American home. Gerhard is about five feet, ten inches tall. He is of fair complexion and stocky build and is employed by the German postal service. Quiet and contemplative, he is keenly interested in spiritual matters and world events as well as the history and chronicles of his community. He makes it a policy to say the blessing not only at the beginning of meals, but also at their conclusion.

Dorothea is, in many ways, the complementing opposite of her husband. She is of medium height, strong, husky, jovial and extremely practical. They own an automobile but Dorothea does the driving which includes taking Gerhard to work. At one time, we were told, she enjoyed riding a motor scooter about the village. Her hobby at the time we were there was the abundant vegetable garden in the yard. Gerhard and Dorothea have two grown daughters who are no longer at home.

While in Wolzhausen I saw again the scenes of the village mentioned in my story. The time there included a visit to the office of the Bürgermeister located in the nearby town of Breidenbach. He presides over a municipality of seven villages which include Wolzhausen. The Bürgermeister, whose name is Artur Künkel, was most gracious and informal during our visit. He came from behind his desk and we all sat in a circle in overstuffed chairs and couches in his spacious office. There were six in our party, the Kochs, Jo and I, Gerhard Becker, and Carmen, Karin Kult's married daughter who helped with the interpreting. For a full hour we discussed events of the past and present. Herr Künkel told us he was eight years old when the Americans arrived. He was not too upset since school was closed for the day!

On the morning of our departure we arose early to drive on to Berlin. A message came, "Before you leave, Karin Kult has something she wants to say to you. Please come to her home.'"

Mrs. Kult had told us already of the sadness of the war years for her and her family. Her father died on the east front in Russia and her mother dressed continually in black.

From left: Paul Koch; Sid Hatch; Artur Künkel, the Bürgermeister; Gerhard Becker of Wolzhaussen

She remembered when the Americans came to Wolzhausen.

We gathered that early morning in Karin Kult's living room, Carmen again helping with the interpreting. "Mother has something to say to you," Carmen said. "She wants to tell you that she doesn't hate American soldiers any more." I got up from the couch on which I was sitting, walked across the room and embraced Karin Kult. For me that was the end of the war.

We walked back up to Gerhard and Dorothea's home and tried to pack our bags into the trunk of the rental car. Combined with souvenirs we had acquired, they would not go in. "Ah, no problem," Dorothea said, and with that she gave everything a big shove and down came the trunk door,

I looked at Dorothea Becker, our hostess for the time we had been there, and I exclaimed, "*Dorothea, du bist wunderbar!*" She laughed heartily and we drove away.

Epilogue: Part B

Memorial Message

During the last few months of writing this book the author was stricken with leukemia. However, in days of remission he gained the mental and physical strength and energy to complete it. He was able to accept the invitation to be Chaplain-speaker at the memorial service of the Blackhawk reunion in San Diego, CA, September 1995.

Sid expressed to his fellow veterans his joy in being able to be present. Indeed, he felt this was the highest honor which had come to him, he told them.

How proud we all were (342nd, Co. E who knew him, and family) as he delivered his message at the reunion — how his strong spirit would not allow his physical condition to hinder his delivery. The straightforwardness that Sid used to convey his testimony of God's supreme goodness and watchcare was most inspirational. Many memories returned!

At the request of not a few Blackhawks present, Sid planned his message to be the epilogue in his book. He also felt it would be a most appropriate finish to the recounting of those combat experiences which had become real spiritual experiences to him for the rest of his life.

This memorial message now has become his final act of service for his country. It is a most fitting close of his life as a witness to his faith, his military service, and his life long ministry.

He joined many other Blackhawk comrades in bivouac just three weeks after he was privileged to deliver the following, his memorial address.

"The Magnificent Agony"

Memorial Message, September 10, 1995, at the Eleventh Annual Reunion of the 86th Blackhawk Division Association, Hanalei Hotel, San Diego, California. By Rev. Sidney A. Hatch (Sgt., Company E, 342nd Infantry).

These men and women whose names have been read this morning were members of a generation that left their homes overnight to answer their country's call. In a few short weeks of basic training they were transformed from private citizens to soldiers in the "Army of the United States." They were in the Army—as we all were—for "the duration and six months." These were the terms we were never allowed to forget.

Now these members of the Blackhawk Association are in bivouac. There they rest until reveille in the morning.

In one of America's early wars, the War with Mexico, 1846-48, there was a terrible battle, the Battle of Buena Vista. Five thousand American troops under Major-General Zachary Taylor were pitted against twenty thousand Mexican troops under General Santa Anna. The American casualties were heavy, over two thousand men were dead, wounded, or missing. In tribute to them, Theodore O'Hara, a member of the U.S. forces, wrote a famous poem, "The Bivouac of the Dead."

I quote only the first stanza.[1]

> The muffled drum's sad roll has beat
> The soldier's last tattoo;
> No more on Life's parade shall meet
> That brave and fallen few.
> On Fame's eternal camping ground
> Their silent tents are spread,
> And Glory guards, with solemn round,
> The bivouac of the dead.

"The bivouac of the dead" is a beautiful figure of speech for the cemetery where each one sleeps in death. It reminds us that our English word "cemetery" comes from the Greek word *koimeterion* meaning a sleeping place.[2] So our fellow Blackhawks, whom we are remembering this morning, are asleep in bivouac until reveille in the morning.

There will be a reveille in the morning, for them and for us, and it won't be just a sergeant's whistle. There will be a real trumpet call, the greatest ever blown.

During my years in seminary I took a special interest in the Old Testament as well as the New. This included five years in the study of Hebrew, the language of the Old testament. I realized then that the Jewish faith has essentially the same future hope as the Christian faith.

King David of Israel said, "I shall be satisfied, when I awake, with thy likeness" (Psalm 17:15). In the beautiful Twenty-third Psalm, with which we are all familiar, David said, "He (the LORD) restoreth my soul" (23:3). I believe in its ultimate sense this means, "Someday the LORD will bring me back to life again."

Finally, there was Daniel who wrote, "And many of them that sleep in the dust of the earth shall awake" (Daniel 12:2).

When we come to the New Testament, the apostle Paul writes in his first letter to the Thessalonian church, "I would not have you to be ignorant ... concerning them which are asleep" (I Thessalonians 4:13). He goes on to tell us: "the Lord himself shall descend from heaven with a shout, with the voice of the archangel, and with the trump of God: and the dead in Christ shall rise first" (I Thessalonians 4:16).

This event described above will be our greatest reunion.

Think of the experiences our fellow Blackhawks carried in their minds and hearts throughout life, and we carry them now: the training in Texas, Louisiana, and California. The long, long train ride from San Luis Obispo to Camp Myles Standish in Massachusetts.

As we went through Kansas City, Missouri, Pfc. James A. Curtis of Company E, 342nd Infantry, could see his home in the distance. He told us later that he felt a strong urge to jump from the train and go home. But he "stuck by the ship." Ironically, Jim Curtis was the first man in our company to die. We stood on a street in Hofolpe, Germany, and watched him breathe his last.

We remember the deep snow in Massachusetts and the cavernous interior of the troop carrier waiting for us in Boston Harbor, the *USS John Erickson*, formerly the Swedish luxury liner *Kungsholm*. As I walked up the gangplank and into that ship I knew how Jonah must have felt when he was swallowed by the whale.

The good Lord and some depth bombs took us safely through the North Atlantic. It was so cold in Normandy at Camp Old Gold that we slept with our boots on. Our accommodations for the train ride from France to the Cologne area were the spacious French freight cars, the historic "Forty and Eights." There were no Pullman cars with plush on the seats and our choice of upper and lower berths. But the floors of those freight cars were covered with straw. We did not complain.

(During that train ride I carried in my pocket a small Hohner "Marine Band" harmonica. In the darkness of the first night I pulled it out of my pocket and began to play. A request then came from S/Sgt. Charles A Stevenson of Washington, D.C. Steve died later in Korea. I'm glad now I played that song for him.)

Our foxholes on the Rhine, the dreaded patrols across the river, the long ride to take up our position on the southeast side of the Ruhr Pocket, the ten days of dark and bloody battle that followed when we watched many of our buddies lay down their lives for the cause we felt was just. These are the days we cannot forget.

After that we traveled south and joined General George S. Patton, one of America's greatest, for the drive across Bavaria. At Ingolstadt we crossed the Danube River under fire, perhaps the most memorable experience of all. Finally, riding on tanks, we rolled into the beautiful green hills of the Austrian Tyrol. There was relief and thanksgiving on our lips as the "German Redoubt" failed to materialize, and perhaps a bit of compassion in our hearts as we received orders, "Don't fire unless fired upon." At that point we waved hundreds of enemy stragglers to the rear.

Then came V-E Day, thirty-day furloughs at home, and after that the trip to the Philippines. By this time we had received many new men into our ranks and once again some of our men saw combat against Japanese hold-outs in the hills and caves of Luzon.

Why review all this? Because I am reminded of Paul's famous words to Timothy, "I have fought a good fight, I have finished my course, I have kept the faith" (II Timothy 4:7).

In the Greek of the New Testament, Paul's word for the phrase, "I have fought" is *agonizomai*. We recognize in it our English word *agonize*. His word for good, *Kalos*, meant "good, excellent, noble, honorable." I like to translate it *Magnificent*. And his word for *fight* is *agon* or *agona* from which comes our word *agony*. My own translation of Paul's famous words is, "I have agonized the magnificent agony." He had been through some terrible experiences, but the nobility of his cause had made it "a magnificent agony."

In many ways the fear and death of combat was an "agony." But with the passing of the years—and the nobility of our cause—it has become "a magnificent agony."

It was an agony made necessary by world affairs at that time. Paul has also written, in his letter to the church at Rome, "If it be possible, as much as lieth in you, live peaceably with all men" (Romans 12:18). But peace was no longer possible in the terrible days of World War II. This verse indicates that there comes a time when men and nations must fight. They have no other choice.

During my years in the ministry I have occasionally had to contend with pacifism. Several years ago a man in Australia wrote me a letter and sent me some material in which he informed me that I could never join his church unless I would confess my "sin" of having served in the military. I wrote back to this man and told him about an experience my wife and I had in New Zealand while on a visit there in 1973.

This was a fraternal visit and preaching mission. When our New Zealand hosts learned that I had served in the military in World War II and even in combat they expressed appreciation. "You don't know how relieved we were," they said, "when American troops arrived in New Zealand during World War II. We knew then we would not become a colony of Japan."

I wrote this to my friend in Australia. I reminded him

that had it not been for the good old USA, his country might have become a colony of Japan. Also, somebody had to fight and die so he could be a pacifist. I received no reply to my letter.

The fallacy of pacifism is two-fold. It fails to recognize that some element of force is necessary to maintain peace and order in the universe. Secondly, it disarms the innocent and leaves them at the mercy of the aggressor and the criminal elements in the world.

Jesus of Nazareth said, in His Sermon on the Mount, "Blessed are the peacemakers; for they shall be called the children of God" (Matthew 5:9). We note that He said "peacemaker," not "peacekeeper." Before peace can be kept, it must be made, even created. That is the role of government, the public official, the soldier, the policeman on the beat. That is why the apostle Paul said, and I apply it to the soldier, "he beareth not the sword in vain: for he is the minister of God, a revenger to execute wrath upon him that doeth evil" (Romans 13:4).

This is what makes the mission of the 86th Infantry Division during World War II almost "a holy cause." As we think back on all we went through at that time, we can remember Paul's words, "I have fought a good fight, I have kept the faith." Or: "I have agonized the magnificent agony."

Many of our fellow Blackhawks are now in bivouac. All of us are awaiting reveille in the morning.

Footnotes
[1] Jessie B. Rittenhouse, ed., *The Little Book of American Poets, 1787-1900* (Boston and New York: Houghton Mifflin Company, 1915), pp. 91-94.
[2] *Encyclopaedia Britannica,* 1954 ed., article "Cemetery," V, 111-13.

Notes

Preface

[1] These words of President John Quincy Adams are taken from John Bartlett, *Familiar Quotations (etc.),* 13th and Centennial ed., completely Revised (Boston, Little, Brown and Company, 1955), p. 398. N.B.: Hereafter references to Bartlett will be abridged.

[2] The reader has no doubt noticed that *Blackhawk* is sometimes spelled as one word and sometimes as two. In this book I prefer the form *Blackhawk*, unless referring to a source.

[3] Philippians 3:13.

[4] Romans 8:28.

[5] Luke 6:35.

Introduction
(A Spiritual Crisis)

[1] Romans 1:31; II Timothy 3:3.

[2] Genesis 45:14-15.

[3] Genesis 46:29.

Chapter 1
How I Became a "Blackhawk"

[1] Richard A. Briggs, *Black Hawks Over the Danube, The History of the 86th Division in Word War II* (West Point, Ky.: Richard A. Briggs, 1954), p. 9.

[2] *The World Book Encyclopedia* (Chicago: Field Enterprises Educational Corporation, 1959), article :"Black Hawk," II, 825-26.

[3] I have heard several times since World War II that the 86th Division was slated to participate in the invasion of Japan. This rumor has been verified for me in recent years.

On Wednesday, August 26, 1992, a letter to the editor appeared in *The Des Moines* (Iowa) *Register* from a Richard W. Peterson of Council Bluffs, Iowa. Mr. Peterson, a member of Company "A" of the 342nd Infantry, wrote that according to information recently released by the Pentagon, the 86th Division was to land in amphibious assault on the island of Honshu east of Tokyo on March 1, 1946.

Mr. Peterson's letter to *The Des Moines Register* was reproduced in the December, 1992, issue of *The Blackhawk Bugle* (Vol.7, No. 4, P. 9), the official magazine of the 86th Blackhawk Division Association of which I am a member.

[4] Jonah 1:15-2:10.

Chapter 2
A Voyage to Uncertainty

[1] Psalm 107:23-24.

[2] This is according to Briggs, *Black Hawks Over the Danube, op.cit.,* p. 24. Mr. Briggs served as a rifleman in Company "I," 342nd Infantry Regiment, 86th Division.

³ *Ibid.*, p. 24. According to Briggs' account, we boarded ship in Boston on February 19, 1945. Our convoy arrived in the harbor of Le Havre, France, on the morning of March 2. We remained on board ship for two more days before disembarking. We were on board ship then for about two weeks.

⁴ I am indebted here not only to my own experience but to the graphic description of the life of an infantryman as found in the article "Infantry" in *Encyclopaedia Britannica* (Chicago: Encyclopaedia Britannica, Inc., 1953), XII, 325-38, especially p. 331. Gen. George C. Marshall reported in 1945 that the United states infantry sustained 70% of all casualties in the nation's armed forces in World War II, though it comprised only one-fifth of the forces overseas. *Ibid.*, p. 331.

N.B.: Hereafter in this book references to *Encyclopaedia Britannica* will be limited to titles, year of edition, volume number and page numbers.

⁵ II Timothy 2:3.

⁶ Psalm 139:7, 9-10.

Chapter 3
"Bon Jour, Monsieur"

¹ S.S. or simply SS became the familiar initials for the German *Schutzstaffel*. *Schutz* meant "protection" or "defense" and *Staffel*, when used in a military sense, meant "echelon" or "detachment." Hence literally Schutzstaffel meant "defense echelon" or "defense detachment." Compare Cassell's German-English, English-German Dictionary, completely revised by Harold T. Betteridge (New York: Macmillan Publishing Company, 1978), pp. 541, 575.

The *Schutztaffel* was actually a paramilitary organization under the National Socialist regime in Germany. However, it was disciplined as a military organization and was one of the special exponents of Nazi doctrine. Compare the article "World War II" in *Encyclopaedia Britannica* (1953 ed.), XXIII, 791B.

[2] Matthew 26:75.

Chapter 4
My Hohner Harmonica
(and the French "Forty and Eights")

[1] Compare Philip A. St. John, Ph.D., *86th Blackhawk Infantry Division* (Paducah, Ky.: Turner Publishing Company, 1992), p. 16.

[2] Ibid., p. 16.

[3] See Chapter 28,. "Ol' Iry from West Virginia (The Man from Strange Creek)."

Chapter 5
Our Foxhole on the Rhine

For this date I am indebted to St. John, *op. cit.*, p. 17, and Briggs, *Black Hawks Over the Danube, op. cit.*, pp. 27-28. Both writers point out that the 86th Division's arrival in Cologne was spread out over a period of several days, March 24-27.

[2] For the information that our specific location was Riehl, I am indebted to Staff Sergeant John F. Wood's account in *"You Ain't Seen Nothin' Yet,"* article *"ETO to Tokyo,"* p.9. This document with its various articles was prepared by men of Company "E" while stationed in the Philippines following the close of hostilities in Europe and Asia. At the time Sgt. Wood (now Dr. Wood) was from Fallows, California. For further remarks regarding *"You Ain't Seen Nothin' Yet,"* see my Preface.

[3] Briggs, *op. cit.*, p. 30.

[4] For these lines I am indebted to John Bartlett, *Familiar Quotations,* 13th and Centennial ed., completely revised (Boston:

Little, Brown and Company, 1955), p. 595. The German original was written by Max Schneckenburger (1819-1849), and its text may be found in Ernst Feise and Harry Steinhauer, eds., *German Literature Since Goethe* (Boston: Houghton Mifflin Company, 1958), p. 114.

⁵ I ask my readers to bear with me if my translation lacks poetic finesse. To be sure I remembered correctly I compared my memory with the German Lines in Feise and Steinhauer, *op. cit.*, p. 16! Happily, my son, Dr. David S. Hatch of Tigard, Oregon, kept his college text book.

⁶ Isaiah 48:18.

⁷ Isaiah 66:12.

⁸ Isaiah 26:3.

⁹ *Gesenius' Hebrew and Chaldee Lexicon to the Old Testament Scriptures,* trans. by Samuel Prideaux Tregelles (Grand Rapids, Michigan: Wm. B. Eerdmans Publishing Company, 1950), p. 825.

¹⁰ St. John, *op. cit.*, p. 17; Briggs, *op. cit.*, p. 31. For a description of the 86th Division's combat experiences in Cologne see both authors: St. John, pp. 16-19, and Briggs, pp. 30-34.

Chapter 6
Crossing the Rhine

¹ The 86th Infantry Division included three infantry regiments, the 341st, 342nd and 343rd. Each regiment included three battalions. Four companies made up a battalion. Also included in the division were cavalry, reconnaissance, engineers, artillery and service units such as headquarters companies, military police, ordnance, quartermaster, signal and medical. Compare St. John, *op. cit.*, p. 10. Also, and not to be overlooked, were the chaplains assigned to the division.

² The identity of the town of Pesch had long ago escaped my memory. I am indebted here to Dr. Wood, *op. cit.*, p. 9.

This assignment for Company "L" was only temporary for during the early morning hours of April 4 the 82nd Airborne Division began to relieve the 86th, unit by unit. By midnight the entire sector was occupied by the 82nd. Compare St. John, *op. cit.*, p. 19.

³ Bonn's cathedral is called the Münster. It stands on the spot where two Roman soldiers were executed in 253 A.D. for their Christian beliefs. I was unaware of this item of Christian history as we passed through the city. Compare Fodor's 90 Germany (New York: Fodor's Travel Publications, Inc., 1990), p. 391.

⁴ Wood, *op. cit.*, p. 10.

⁵ Deuteronomy 23:12-14.

Chapter 7
The Village I Could not Forget
(Part One)

¹ In later years I would learn that this little stream was called "the Perf." It was a tributary to the River Lahn which flowed into the Rhine. How I acquired this information is a story to be told before the conclusion of this book.

² These guests, as I have called them, were probably refugees from the east. This too I learned in later years.

Chapter 8
The Village I Could Not Forget
(Part Two)

¹ Romans 11:29.

² I Corinthians 12:27.

³ Ephesians 4:3.

⁴ I Chronicles 12:32.

⁵ Revelation 11:15, more literal translation.

⁶ Galatians 3:26.

[7] William Cowper's beautiful words may be found in many Christian Hymnals. They are: "God moves in a mysterious way, His wonders to perform; He plants his footsteps in the sea, and rides upon the storm."

Chapter 9
Some Background for Blessings in Hell

[1] Bartlett, *op. cit.*, p. 613.

[2] Wood, *op. cit.*, p. 10.

[3] Richard A. Briggs, *The Battle of the Ruhr Pocket, A Combat Narrative* (West point, Ky.: Richard A. Briggs, 1957), pp. 12, 26.

[4] Ibid., pp. 25-26.

[5] Ibid., p. 9.

[6] Wood, *op. cit.*, p. 11

[7] Briggs, *Black Hawks Over the Danube, op. cit.*, p. 37.

[8] Ezekiel 34:12

[9] Both quotations are in Bartlett, *op. cit.*, p. 613.

Chapter 10
Jim's Courage

[1] The Baptist General Conference of America.

[2] Vol. 8, No. 2, pp. 10-11.

[3] Romans 11:34.

[4] John 11:25.

[5] For this amplification of Jesus' words in John 11:25, I am indebted to E. W. Bullinger, *Figures of Speech Used in the Bible: Explained and Illustrated* (New York: E. & J. B. Young & Co., 1898), p. 562. It is my understanding that this venerable reference work has been republished by Baker Book House in Grand Rapids, Michigan.

Chapter 11
"Du Bist Wie Eine Mutter
(You Are Like a Mother")*

[1] As indicated in the Preface, I first told this story of the wounded German soldier who said, "Du bist wie eine Mutter," in an article entitled, "The Night I Overcame My Enemy," which appeared in *Sunday Digest* for September 5, 1965, published by David C. Cook Publishing Company of Elgin Illinois (850 N. Grow Ave., 60120). It is told here again (with some changes) with their permission.

[2] I do not have the information as to Pat Gallagher's home town and State. This was not the last time he would treat German wounded. Later, at Pfunz in Bavaria, he would treat them again. Wood, *op. cit.*, p. 13.

[3] Matthew 5:7.

[4] Romans 12:20.

Chapter 12

Hands Upon Shoulders in the Darkness
(And a Mission of Mercy in the Morning)

[1] Psalm 139:5, 11.

[2] In Psalm 139:11 the Hebrew word for "cover" is *shuph*. The Gesenius-Tregelles lexicon suggests that in the context of this verse it means "fall upon" or "overwhelm." *Gesenius' Hebrew and Chaldee Lexicon to the Old Testament Scriptures [etc.]* translated by Samuel Prideaux Tregelles (Grand Rapids, Michigan: Wm. B. Eerdmans Publishing Company, 1950), p. 811.

Chapter 13
The Slaughter of the Cooks

[1] I am not sure of Wallace Stasielowski's home town or city in Massachusetts.

[2] My friend and buddy in combat, Dr. John F. Wood, was with the captain when he came out of the ditch and seized the horse by the bridle.

[3] This story is recorded in II Samuel 16:5-14.

[4] II Samuel 3:1.

[5] II Samuel 16:11.

[6] I Samuel 16:7; Matthew 23:27; John 7:24; II Corinthians 10:7.

[7] Romans 3:23.

Chapter 14
"I Will to Go Home!"
(The God-given Instinct)

[1] Bartlett, *op. cit.*, p 464.

[2] Of those who gave their lives for their country, the names available to me are: James N. Curtis, Jr. (Kansas City, MO), Nelson R. Davis (Hillsboro, NH), Thomas A. Hastie, and Charles S. Wilson (Texas). I regret that I do not know Thomas Hastie's home town and State.

Staff Sergeant Joseph A. Carrier of Brownsville, Kentucky, and Master Sergeant Steve Szobota of Brooklyn, New York, received battlefield commissions. Harry M. Gianlorenzo of Providence, Rhode Island, and James N. Curtis, Jr., received the Silver Star, the latter posthumously. Twenty-five recipients of the Purple Heart and ten recipients of the Bronze Star are listed in *"You Ain't Seen Nothin' Yet,"* *op. cit.* In several instances, men received more than one award.

The information in this note is taken from the booklet, *"You Ain't Seen Nothin' Yet," op. cit.*

[3] John Heisy's home town in Pennsylvania is unknown to me.

[4] Luke 9:58, compare also Matthew 8:20. For this thought I am indebted to Ralph W. Sockman, *Exposition of the First Book of Kings,* in *The Interpreter's Bible* (New York and Nashville: Abingdon Press, 1954), III, 53.

[5] Compare the remarks in *Ibid.*, p. 52.

Chapter 15
Hohenlimburg: The Choir on the Hill

[1] Briggs, *Black Hawks Over the Danube, op. cit.,* p. 58. Quoted with permission.

[2] I borrow the thought from George Eliot's (Mary Ann Evans') poem, "The Choir Invisible." The poem may be found in Roy J. Cook, compiler, *One Hundred and One Famous Poems; With a Prose Supplement.* rev. ed. (Chicago: The Reilly & Lee Co., 1958), pp. 137-38.

[3] St. John, *op. cit.*, p. 27.

[4] *Ibid.*, p. 27.

[5] I Corinthians 2:14.

Chapter 17
My Ambulance to Bavaria

[1] Proverbs 20:1

[2] Briggs, *Black Hawks Over the Danube, op. cit.*, p. 61.

[3] *Ibid.*, p. 62

[4] *Ibid.*, pp. 62-63

[5] *Ibid.*, p. 64

[6] *Ibid.*, p. 64.

Chapter 18
The Attack on Ingolstadt
(with Music in the Afternoon)

[1] *Baedeker's Germany*, article "Ingolstadt" (New York, N.Y.: Prentice Hall Trade Division, n.d.), p. 157.

[2] Briggs, *Black Hawks Over the Danube, op, cit.*, p. 71.

[3] *Ibid.*, p. 74.

[4] *Encyclopaedia Britannica, op. cit.*, article "Ingolstadt," XII, 352.

[5] Briggs, *op. cit.*, p. 77. According to Briggs' account the fort was located two miles inland from the river. However, the fort which we entered, and which we understood at the time had been secured by "G" Company, was located just above the river. During our 1982 visit only a street separated it from the river.

Chapter 19
Death in a Garden of Roses
(A Parable of Mankind)

[1] Wood, *op, cit.*, p.14.

[2] Genesis 3:1-24

[3] Matthew 26:36-39.

[4] John 19:41

[5] Revelation 21:4.

Chapter 20
The Soldier's Prize
(and the Hungarians)

[1] Psalm 119:162.

[2] Franz Delitzsch, *Biblical Commentary on the Psalms*, trans. from the German (from the 2nd ed., revised throughout) by the

Rev. Francis Bolton (Grand Rapids, Michigan: Wm B. Eerdmans Publishing Company, 1952), III, 262.

Chapter 21
An Encounter with the Geneva Convention
(My Hardest Job in Combat)

[1] Bartlett, *op. cit.*, p.110.

[2] Brenau College, Gainesville, Georgia, class of 1907.

[3] *Encyclopaedia Britannica, op. cit.*, article "Barracks," III, 135-138.

[4] *The World Book Encyclopedia, op. cit.*, article "Geneva Conventions" VII, 2906.

Chapter 22
The Password Incarnate
(Lost in a Snow Storm)

[1] Briggs describes this day and storm in his book, *Black Hawks Over the Danube, op. cit.,* pp. 88-89. He gives May 1, 1945, as the date of the snow storm.

[2] John 1:14, 10:7, 14:6.

Chapter 24
On the Banks of the Salzach River
("I Can't Get My Breath")

[1] The 86th Infantry Division became known as the "Kid Division." According to Briggs, the average age of the entire division, officers and all, was twenty-two years. *Black Hawks Over the Danube, op. cit.,* p. 7 in the Foreword.

[2] I am indebted to Dr. John F. Wood for this personal account

of what happened on the road while our squad was located up the bank of the river.

[3] Dr. Wood has also related to me these events surrounding Kelly's return to the company.

Chapter 25
Arrival in an Austrian Village
(A "Friend" from California)

[1] Matthew 5:7

Chapter 26
The Old Mill and the Miller
(A Good Place for Combat to End)

[1] Compare the account in Alfred B. Smith, *Al Smith's Treasury of Hymn Histories* (Montrose, Pennsylvania: Heritage Music Distributors, Inc. copyright 1982 by Alfred B, Smith), pp. 289-92.

[2] See St. John, *op. cit.*, p. 28. Also Briggs, *Black Hawks Over the Danube, op cit.* p.64.

Chapter 27
"Haben Sie Eier?"
("Have You Any Eggs?" Reflections on Eating During Combat)

[1] "Marmalade" in German is pronounced with four syllables, "Mar-ma-la-de."

[2] John 6:35, 48.

[3] Wood, *op.cit.*, p.15.

[4] The Hebrew word is *'eseb* which refers to "greens" in the sense of "food for men." See Ludwig Koehler, ed., *Lexicon in*

Veteris Testamenti Libros (Grand Rapids, Michigan: Wm. B. Eerdmans Publishing Company, 1953), p. 739.

Chapter 28
Ol' Iry from West Virginia
(The Man from Strange Creek)

[1] See St. John, *op. cit.*, p. 12.

[2] These phrases are from the King James Version of the Bible. See Joshua 1:14; I Chronicles 5:24; Genesis 6:4, and other passages.

[3] For this account of Ira's experiences at Morro Bay, I am indebted to the chapter entitled "Heaven on Earth" which is included in the booklet, *"You Ain't Seen Nothin' Yet,"* *op. cit.*, pp. 6-8. This chapter describes our training at San Luis Obispo and Morro Bay. It was written by one of our Company "E" buddies, S.Sgt. Robert M. Chase, now a graduate engineer (retired) in Hampden, Maine.

[4] For those who do not recall "Willie and Joe," I refer them to Bill Mauldin's book, *Up Front* (New York: Henry Holt and Company, 1943), 228 pages.

[5] Luke 24:13-35.

[6] Psalm 37:23-24.

Chapter 29
Return to Heddesheim

[1] This is my own free translation of Proverbs 10:7.

[2] Psalm 139:9.

[3] I could never remember the exact length of time we were in Heddesheim, thinking it was close to three weeks. But Dr. Wood, *op. cit.*, p. 16, says it was seventeen days. I have no doubt that he is correct.

[4] Philippians 4:8.

Chapter 30
A Day We Laid Our Rifles Down
(A Parable of the Future)

[1] Briggs, *Black Hawks Over the Danube, op. cit.*, p. 44.
[2] Isaiah 2:4.
[3] Isaiah 9:6.
[4] II Timothy 2:11-12.
[5] II Corinthians 5:19-20

Chapter 31
The Impartiality of Suffering

[1] Compare the Moffatt Bible's translation of I Corinthians 1:26-28.
[2] Matthew 5:5.

Epilogue-Part A
(Wolzhausen:1990)

[1] The weekly newspaper in which my story of Wolzhausen appeared was called *Wochenseitung für die Gemeinde Breidenbach.* The date was Friday, November 10, 1989, pp. 8-9. The story was carried again in the issue of May 4, 1990, pp. 5-6.